# GODDIE

Trish

Goddie is all of us!

Thank you!

11/21

RJS

## WHAT PEOPLE ARE SAYING
## ABOUT *GODDIE*

"Biographical novels are at times a Machiavellian tool used to 'humble-brag' about the main subject. *Goddie* is the antithesis of this. Robert Picart is masterful at painting a picture and capturing the moment. He describes events with such accuracy the reader will believe the lyrical illusion and feel exactly what he wants to convey. In *Goddie*, Picart wove a West Indian journey that forces those of us born to immigrant parents to take stock, stand proud, and commit to finishing the vision for which our forebears sacrificed."

— DONALD F. MCLEOD
CHILDHOOD FRIEND &
JUSTICE IN THE ONTARIO COURT OF JUSTICE

"I saw my mother's life and heard my grandmother's voice in the poetic and melodious writing of *Goddie*. This profound, emotional, and beautiful story is my people's narrative. Each page stirred a visceral reaction that kept me with her every step of the way."

"The students I see every day are worthy descendants of the powerful legacies that Goddie's story represents. This novel is a moment for teenagers to see the voyage of many Black families in contemporary literature."

"The first few lines I read from *Goddie* took my breath away. Picart's lyrical writing and lush imagery transports readers immediately into Goddie's life and takes you on a journey that will leave you amazed and breathless at the end. By the time you are done, you too will believe that anything is possible."

"Picart's profound and expressive writing left me bursting with curiosity about my capacity to be resilient. The endless unboxing of characters, friends or foes, drew me into Goddie's inspiring world full of sights, sounds, nostalgic warm breezes and unbridled hope."

"This book provides an intimate window into the life of Goddie and her life's journey through an exploration of the personal interruptions of life, loss, trauma, birth, perseverance, and hope. Her story brilliantly captures the lesser-known history of the movement of Black women during the mid-20th century from places in the English-speaking Caribbean like Jamaica to England and to Canada in pursuit of a better life for themselves and their families. *Goddie* is a welcomed contribution to Black Canadian literature."

— NATASHA HENRY, PRESIDENT, ONTARIO BLACK HISTORY SOCIETY

"An intriguing read, *Goddie* was like a mirror that reminded me that extraordinary circumstances produce extraordinary people."

— SHARON RILEY, JUNO AND HARRY JEROME AWARD-WINNING VOCALIST AND MUSIC EDUCATOR.

"*Goddie* brought to life the trials, tribulations, and triumphs of every Black mother. A constant mix of blues and jubilation, her vivid life illustrates how brutal circumstances can transform and elevate us to a place where eventually the journey all makes sense. The pearl-like words of Goddie's story will bring tears to your eyes and warmth to your heart."

— DAHABO AHMED-OMER, EXECUTIVE DIRECTOR OF THE BLACKNORTH INITIATIVE

"The story of *Goddie* is a searing tribute to the people of Jamaica and the wider Caribbean diaspora. Picart beautifully wove a solemn tale of loss and abandonment against the backdrop of my home country. This story brought to life all the conversations my mother and father shared with me growing up. *Goddie* is a celebration and a worthy catalyst for discussion with my students. Picart has done us all a service."

— MARLA HUNTER, PROFESSOR OF MATHEMATICS
AND SCIENCE, JOHN HOPKINS UNIVERSITY OF EDUCATION

"*Goddie* masterfully captures a familiar journey of many Jamaican immigrants with grace and reverence. Robert Picart colourfully salutes a riveting woman's testimony of overcoming significant odds in the pursuit of a better life. A magnificent contribution to understanding the untold chronicles of Caribbean people who paved the road for people like me to travel."

— LENWORTH (LEN) CARBY,
UNITED WAY GREATER TORONTO TRUSTEE

"*Goddie* is an inspiring story of a young woman's search for her place in the world. With a moving narrative of love, surviving loss, friendship, strength, and hope, she invites the reader into her deepest contemplations and draws you to the refreshing sights and sounds of "home". Robert Picart craftily depicts the tumultuous journey across the sea, and connects us all to the true historical footprint of so many Jamaican people. It renews the strength and perseverance of a culture who have made some of the greatest contributions to Canadian life. *Goddie* will make wonderful addition to any curriculum."

— MICHELLE FRANCIS,

EDUCATOR AND CURRICULUM CONSULTANT

"Picart paints a colourful and complex picture of the life of Caribbean people that goes well beyond the typical, two-dimensional storytelling of our experience that so often populates popular media and entertainment. *Goddie* is necessary reading for those interested in truly understanding the grit, strength, and character of Jamaican people—on and off the island, and for those interested in knowing the stories that were never fully revealed to us by those who forged the path for us."

— KIMBERLY BENNETT,

DIRECTOR OF COMMUNICATIONS,

CANADIAN RACE RELATIONS FOUNDATION

"Robert Picart's vivid language instantly transported me into Goddie's world and took me on a ride I didn't want to end! Her sheer courage to push through and persevere is inspiring. As a child of island soil, I know the often painful truth of the past can cause stories to never be told. Goddie's truth created a deep longing to know my family's history better!"

— STACY CAMPBELL MARSHALL,

"DAY IN THE LIFE OF AN ISLAND WIFE"

LIFESTYLE VLOGGER, NASSAU, BAHAMAS

# GODDIE

ROBERT PICART

NEW DEGREE PRESS

GODDIE

*This is a work of creative non-fiction. Some parts have been
fictionalized in varying degrees, for various purposes.*

*Permission requests: www.robertpicart.com*

*Unless otherwise indicated, Bible verses are taken from the
following translation: King James Version (KJV), Public Domain.*

*Cover art by SirIsrael Azariah King. @siakoriginals*
*Cover design by Bojana Gigovska*

Published by New Degree Press

First Edition: 2022

Library of Congress Control Number: 2021917813

ISBN
978-1-63730-431-0   *Paperback*
978-1-63730-519-5   *Kindle Ebook*
978-1-63730-520-1   *Digital Ebook*

## TO MY MOTHER, VETA

*You gave us everything. You did it alone.*

*You never complained. You never gave up.*

*I just wanted you to see yourself.*

*I hope you like it.*

# CONTENTS

—

*Fear thou not; for I am with thee: be not dismayed; for I am thy God: I will strengthen thee; yea, I will help thee; yea, I will uphold thee with the right hand of my righteousness.*

—ISAIAH 41:10

—KING JAMES VERSION

# FOREWORD

———

We don't really know anyone, now do we? We think we do. We search the world looking for heroes to rescue us, generals to lead us, and bishops to teach us. We do all this not knowing the greatest mystery could be sitting right in front of us, stirring her English tea.

Sure, Robert and I knew the caregiver and provider. But we didn't really know her at all. Good Jamaican manners would say we call her "Mum," but her family nicknamed her Goddie. For Robert and me, this person stirring her tea was a stranger.

The revelations started with the simple inquiry: "Tell us about your childhood." Robert's original plan was to record a few stories for a podcast or maybe just keep for our kids. In exchange, we both received a gift.

Going on this writing journey with Robert has been amazing. As his twin brother, I can't express how proud I am. Watching him write about the life of Goddie has taught me that a reverent separation happens when you capture your parent's experience. You listen like a child, but you gather facts as an investigator. It's not enough to just sling sentences together. You have to get it right.

Robert wanted to ensure it was all meaningfully articulated. His inexperience as an author would hold no water to the magnitude of this moment. Watching him empty his emotions and rise intellectually was inspiring.

As we sat and listened, she would look to the left and take herself back to a time when no shoes, four to a bed, and outdoor kitchens were the norm. Her voice rambled as she detailed the trauma of parental death, loneliness, and heartbreak. While it is the job of our elders to share their lessons, it isn't their job to relive their traumas for our consumption. Even in writing this, I'm humbled deeply at the privilege to watch Robert interpret this for her.

The protective side of my mother said that watching her father die, burying her mother six months later, and becoming indentured all at sixteen was nobody's business. It was her cross to bear.

West Indians are renowned for their secrets and ferocious about privacy. As Robert concentrated on the stories of escape, heartbreak, migration, and depression, we both realized that this was not just a conversation. It was a masterclass in how to navigate your life when it keeps getting interrupted.

When you realize the backdrop to this story takes place in the country hills of Jamaica, the dichotomy really comes to life. Who knew the land of jerk chicken, white rum, and reggae music was capable of inflicting so much trauma? Jamaica had everything. For Goddie, everything wasn't anything.

As the conversations with mum got deeper and the hours got longer, Robert and I realized what she was sharing wasn't just for us to hoard. The lessons were much deeper and much richer.

Robert wrote this novel based on Goddie's story for any person who's ever had to start life over. For some, it is not just in the starting; it's in the starting over from the middle of wherever you are. Only a few get to start over from the beginning. The rest of us pick up the fragments and start from the middle.

The journey of this novel meets the reader who lives at the crossroads of aspiration and anguish. Goddie's story is about her journey through trauma and misdeed—a life that winds its way through the coffee hills of Blue Mountain and the district of Spring Hill. A life that digs deep into the sinew of Jamaica and examines a time not so far removed from slavery.

It was a time when classes ruled the masses, and simplicity and gratefulness were the tools of war. Goddie's story examines the potency of Jamaican culture through the lens of loss and discovery. Witness the granular transition of a poor girl learning how to recover again, again, and again.

This novel is more than a story. This novel is us.

It now serves as a lighthouse, warning us against the missteps of the past while giving us the insight to see ourselves and where we come from. Although this story is emotional, it serves to remind us all that victory lives in each foot we put in front of the other.

Robert started down the path of a motivational memoir, but the journey took on a bigger meaning. It became clear her life lessons could be applied to anyone's journey. Writing a novel based on her life allowed him to underscore the fundamental themes of resiliency and triumph in the midst of upheaval.

Robert and I send encouragement to all those who read this and hope this inspires you to keep going. Please understand that it is possible to redefine who you are. If a young girl alone in the world can start over with nothing but a bag and a boat ticket, then you can start over too. You'll be okay. You can start your interrupted life over from the middle.

It's not over. Keep pressing.

Richard Picart

# PART I

# MORNING BREEZE

# CHAPTER 1

# MORNING BREEZE

---

The morning breeze was a false friend.

The breeze from the southwest wound its way through the parish, embracing everyone willing to meet it. It cut across the farms and hit the faces of Spring Hill with the promise of renewal. Spring Hill was a small district town in the mountains of Jamaica. The morning breeze jumped from hut to house and from churchyard to farmyard.

It teased all to venture out and seek the promise of the day. The morning breeze woke the lush eastern parish. The trees rose for duty, the rivers announced their presence, and the sun assumed the overseer position once held by others.

Warm and thick with promise, the morning breeze carried with it the fragrance of fried dumplings and fresh ackee. Salt air washed the terror of the past, the grief of yesterday, and for some, the promise of tomorrow.

In 1945, the island of Jamaica was divided into fourteen parishes that spanned three hundred square miles. In the far east, the Portland parish was home to Blue Mountain. The mountain held the Spring Hill district in its bosom, giving it the best of everything and nothing. Some described it as more beautiful than any woman.

If Portland was beautiful, then Spring Hill was its daughter—perfect and imperfect at the same time. This world in the hills offered a poor man's Eden, a rebuke of the changing nearby Port Antonio. The bush forgave everyone and no one as it offered both medicine and restriction in its duties.

Once governed by the Arawak people, Jamaica gave up her seed to adopt new seed from Africa. Nigerian sinew now carved her glory. She soon scattered her African seed only to allow new seed from China and India to take hold. The strength required to survive the depression caused Jamaica to war against herself, trading slave owners for political parties. Jamaicans had grown accustomed to the turmoil.

Portland was the place of runaway slaves. Freedom fighters and rebellion forces made their home there. Like stubborn iron, Jamaicans forged their beauty from the battles waged one hundred years prior.

In the 1800s, it was said Jamaica held the worst of the enslaved. The island watched as prophets became pickers, kings traded crowns for scars, and noblemen bowed to the sugar cane. Palaces turned into plantations, and the bellies of ships traded lots for the blue of the ocean. Those who refused to bow would bend or be buried.

The new Jamaicans were now unwilling citizens without a passport. The old religion of tribe and deity traded lots for the quiet belief in freedom. This freedom morphed from reality to principles and goals. Simple freedom was no longer an only child. It now had the siblings of political, intellectual, and spiritual freedom. If freedom was the goal, then initiative and ambition were the keys and long-suffering was the price.

The sun seared Jamaica's soul into its people. Dark skin baked to perfection encased muscular bodies capable of doing anything. Yam and dasheen roots fed the will to move gracefully from era to era, making the impossible seem easy while defying the circumstances surrounding them.

Slavery couldn't shave away their high cheek bones, long limbs, and sturdy stature. Magnificence came from their pores and glistened on their scalp like a crown. Brilliance illuminated their eyes, and artistry was their currency. Jamaicans could do anything, cook anything, grow anything, and suffer anything.

Post-slavery Jamaicans didn't seek pity; they sought to be released to claim their potential, unguarded and unsupervised. Jamaica's greatest crop was its people—people who would gladly trade the suffrage of the sun for the winter of new beginnings. For some, the winter was found in the hills of Portland, Jamaica.

For one young girl, it all began in the hills of Portland in 1945.

Surviving in 1945 was hard. Surviving in Jamaica was relentless. Surviving in Jamaica meant enslavement by circumstance. The work was uncompromising. There was never a break. The flux of life was determined by powers incapable of measure.

For the Ormsby family, the flux of life was determined by two things. What they could grow, and what they could sell. This was Jamaica. This was Portland. This was Spring Hill.

Yes, the morning breeze was a false friend. For one little girl named Goddie, the August breeze of 1945 would never feel the same again.

# CHAPTER 2

# GODDIE

———

The morning was the best time for Goddie because it was the only time her imagination held center court uninterrupted.

While lying in bed looking out the window, she could see the palm overseers. They swayed back and forth, mocking her for sleeping in. The distraction was enough to forget the two other people lying beside her and the little one at her feet.

As she lay on her back, the dichotomy of her life was as simple as shifting her eyes from the tin roof to the open blue skies. She was a poor girl living on a paradise island. The sun pierced through the rusted metal edges of the roof. Even though the sun's presence meant work, it also meant new mercies.

Goddie was happy. In 1945, most Jamaicans were happy, but poor. Dirt poor. It was almost a birthright. Her family paid their land rent and ate much of what they farmed. They sold what they could and remained faithful over the rest. They knew it could be much worse. Much, much, worse.

She was the middle child of nine. It was a brood of sorts, spanning ages over twenty years. The clan started with the eldest son Lambert and made its way down to Edith, the baby.

Goddie had her charge of the younger ones while the oldest four worked the farm, the house, and inevitably, the war.

Her dreams demanded high detail and more room. A three-room house with eleven people was not enough room for all her glory. Goddie's ideas spread wide and spared none. They bore more weight than her bed frame could handle. Her dreams could not be secured by a simple wooden slat and roaming dog. There had to be more than fighting four people in a one-man bed. There just had to be more than putting in a day's work before eight o'clock.

She looked forward to the mornings. That's when she reviewed her game plan. Her training began long before the school bell, and the fight stretched far beyond the island. For her, the early morning was the chance to prepare for the day's challenges. She checked her body, her mind, and her spirit. Hard life had already taken enough, and she was not giving up anymore.

"Goddie! I'm not cleaning up for you again! Yuh can deal with Daadie this time. It's time yuh backside get warm up now," shouted Lauretta, Goddie's oldest sister, who never shied away from letting the world know.

"I'm coming. I'm coming," acquiesced Goddie as she snapped back to reality and Spring Hill's gravity. Dreaming would have to wait until later.

"Lassie Ormsby, get up now. You too, Minnette. Go wash yuh face before Mumma come. Come on!" barked Goddie.

Sharing a bed with three siblings was a hardship, especially in the mornings. Goddie became a sergeant, as she wanted no part of dealing with the general. Daadie was kind, but he did not play around with the morning routine.

"Ok, I'm sending Daadie for you. You all will move faster then," Lauretta said as she turned to leave. "A good switch will make things all clear. Keep going. Yuh doing fine." She stormed off again and swung the door open to find her father.

"Get up, nuh?" Goddie complained, shoving Minnette from the bed in retaliation. "Yuh should know by now. It's school time. Stop pretend. LET'S GO."

As she climbed out of her bed and looked for her uniform, she realized her dreams, for now, would have to be exchanged for reality. Duty called, and it was only calling once. Get these kids ready or deal with Daadie.

The Ormsby family lived in a simple district. There was the school, the church, the graveyard, and the post office. That was Spring Hill in Portland, Jamaica. Everything else was subject to the imagination.

Goddie knew imagination itself would have to be deferred for washing faces, washing floors, and wiping furniture all before school. Crisp uniforms. Bodies fed. Books in hand. No exceptions. She pushed the last sibling out of the room and slid into view of the broken mirror on the wall.

Goddie believed she was beautiful. She was the reflection of both the trial and triumph of Portland, Jamaica. She was forever long. Her arms were limbs and her legs flowed. For sixteen, she was towering. All nine children of Christopher and Caroline Ormsby stretched toward the sky as if growing their way out of poverty was an option.

Everything about her was long. Her arms wrapped around her as if she was her only friend. Her fingers encased everything she touched. Her lashes took their time to recover when she gazed. Her hands were like unworn English gloves. They were delicate enough to finish a braid and strong enough to fill the water drum before school.

Goddie was more personified than even she knew. Her high cheek bones and pronounced lips certified her blackness, but her stride certified her queendom. Everything leads to the eyes. They were indifferent. They dissected the reality of Portland with ease and showed no partiality. Always shifting slowly, they recorded everything on film to be assessed and decided later.

The eyes were the lieutenants, and they always reported the truth. There would be no verdict in the moment—only the collection of truths and hard lessons that would bear fruit later. She knew she was a queen, but royalty was rarely recognized in its own land.

"Yes, keep staring in the mirror. Mumma soon come," Delvina whispered. Goddie turned to throw daggers but quickly looked back at the mirror. Delvina was her birth name, but everyone called her Dearis. Dearis came after Goddie in age but spoke as the elder in the bedroom. "The pretty looks dun, and yuh nuh get none." She laughed and bounded out the room for breakfast and inspection.

Dearis didn't seem to have dreams. Not like Goddie's anyway. Her dreams were limited to getting the last dumpling, kissing Mumma goodbye, and running out to the road to meet schoolmates before they left her.

Goddie rubbed coconut oil all over her long arms and legs. It made her cocobolo hair color shine and her skin beautiful. She oiled herself not only to protect herself from the sun, but also to protect herself from life. She had to preserve herself as much as possible. Sheen was the protection. It was a foolish protection perhaps, but Goddie was clear. She did not want what was around her to get in.

She was saving room for more, saving room for what the swaying coconut trees and morning breeze had promised. If a little bit of coconut oil ensured she would see more, she would have dumped the whole can over her head.

Goddie took on many roles as the middle child. Her impatience grew as she felt stuck resolving fights among older ones and having to explain it all to the younger ones. She got away with a lot but was smart enough to know tall people can't hide forever.

She quickly threw her uniform over her head, brushed off the front, and headed out of the room.

# CHAPTER 3

# DAADIE

---

The days drifted into weeks as the school term made its way through the early summer.

Goddie always had so much to do before heading off to school. The only part she enjoyed was sweeping up. The thrush of the brush broom was meditative. There was something about moving the broom from side to side. Like a metronome, it relaxed the tensions of life and cleared her mind to focus on other things.

With all the siblings outside, she was free to sweep quickly. Goddie fixed the plaits in her hair and started sweeping from the back of the house, working the rooms one by one.

Her housedress swayed in the rhythm as the open windows flushed the dust out with the morning breeze. With the front door open, she could see clear into the field. There she saw a familiar figure coming toward her. She didn't want Daadie to see her, so she looked through the wood slats of the house and watched him. Watching Daadie walk in from the fields became a morning ritual.

The sun preceding his silhouette was careful not to let him fall. It was strange because he never stumbled. He never fell. Even the oxen buckled from time to time, but not him.

Although the ridges of the plowed field were high, and the rocks and tree roots commanded respect, he always walked straight. He knew every inch of that land. He stepped on rocks and roots like a skipping rock on a quiet lake. Like an inspector, he scanned every leaf, every root, and every sucker, looking for any sign of disobedience to the cause.

For some reason, the sun never affected Daadie the way it affected everyone else. He could stay in the field longer, sweat slower, see farther, and smile bigger. He was forever happy in his heart. He knew he was blessed.

The creases of life gave way to the smile on his face. Hard life had carved its mark and shaped his eyes. His grey hair gave notice to time, but the rest of his body held on to the secret. His smile wasn't perfect, but it was perfect to her. He was always glad to see his middle daughter. Goddie reminded him of his own mother.

Goddie continued to watch her father walk toward the house. As he came closer, his strides become stronger and longer. She swept her way out to the veranda to see him better.

Goddie remembered the Genesis story where God told Adam he would toil all the days of his life. Daadie was Adam. Nothing was given to him. Even the land he toiled would mock him forever. As he walked up, excitement replaced exhaustion. Before walking up to the house, he always looked back at the field. It was like he was warning the fields to behave in his absence.

*Daadie looks tired already, and it's not even midday,* Goddie thought to herself. She kept her concerns quiet and quickly got back to sweeping.

As the grinding rocks gave notice of his approach, Goddie filled with pride. There were only a few moments between breakfast and the school bell, and she wasn't about to waste any of them. She situated herself on the step, like she did most mornings, just waiting for her chance to have him to herself.

His words were better than food. They had more nutrients than yams, were sweeter than bananas, and had more fiber than any fruit she could have. Spending time with Daadie was spending time in school before school. The fundamentals of arithmetic and spelling had their place, but the words of her father had their mark.

"Yuh nyam breakfast already?" he asked quietly before straightening a water jug. Daadie was about order. Everything around him had to be done properly and in order. Even the water jug was subject to correction.

"Yuh get Reynold ready? 'im always di late one," he said as he sat down. Reynold was the youngest boy. His nickname was Foot, but Goddie preferred Reynold instead.

"Yes, Daadie," Goddie replied. "'im eating now wid Dearis an' Minnette. Mumma serve di porridge gi 'im."

"Yuh uniform look gud, Goddie. It's always important fe look presentable. Yuh can't become sumting if yuh nuh luk like sumting. Yuh memba yuh Bible verse from yesterday?" he asked.

"Di fear of di Lord ah di beginning of wisdom an di knowledge of di holy understanding," she looked across and said. Goddie was so tall there was no looking up, only looking across. He didn't mind. He knew he was training a giant, and giants never look up.

She reached over and brushed sugar cane fragments from his pant leg. She could feel his knees were swollen as she brushed the cane away. He never complained about the pain in his knees. Still, Goddie knew his body was breaking down. Her thoughts were broken when he cleared his throat.

"What's the rest of the verse?" he said.

"Proverbs nine, verse ten," she replied. Goddie knew her verses. She would not be tested. He half-smiled at his student and stood up.

Daadie instructed the older ones to take care of the younger ones, and the younger ones to heed the older ones. He created rules and structure, and they followed. Other children suffered the absence of their father to war, so the Ormsby children knew the treasure they had.

He was impatient with laziness and never suffered fools long. Goddie was lucky enough not to see the switch very often. She knew that doing her part was helping the family do their part, and helping the family do their part was helping Daadie do his part longer.

He sat back down and looked out. "Goddie, I will nuh always be 'ere. Commit God's word tuh yuh heart an yuh wi neva fail," he instructed.

"Yes, sir," she replied. Goddie tossed around some small rocks with her feet as she listened. He only said a few words that morning. She could tell his knees were hurting, but he would never confess that.

Survival was the war, and pain was the price. Goddie knew the curve in his back was symbolic of the bridge they all walked on toward better things. Like many of the trellis bridges in Spring Hill, they looked weak, but they carried many from nowhere to somewhere. Even if the somewhere was nowhere.

"It's time fi me to go, Daadie," Goddie said, brushing off her backside where she sat and gathering her things.

Daadie was detailed in how the crops were plowed, how the fields were maintained, and how the harvest was organized. He organized both the loading of the produce in the morning and the accounting of the fields at night. Stopping was dying, so he worked. He was the elder of the district and held court to resolve any issues that arose in the community. Goddie never saw him riding. He was always walking and singing a hymn quietly to himself. He would walk down Spring Hill Road to the post office and check for any news from the Farm Bureau.

Daadie's life was his crops. He could grow anything in anything. He cultivated the biggest and most hearty yams. He made the sweetest bananas. He farmed the best fruit. Everyone in the Farm Bureau knew his coffee crop. Coffee paid the bills. Coffee paid the school fee, and coffee paid for the uniforms. He taught Goddie the coloration of the beans and when to pick them. He was a perfectionist. He demanded excellence from his children and excellence from his crops. He always got both.

He was the policeman, the politician, the pastor, and the parent.

Goddie grew up watching Mumma love Daadie. She was forever staring at him. Forever listening to him. Forever hanging off his every word. Mumma knew that if Daadie said it, then it was so. Daadie was wise enough to listen as well, and they worked together to rear nine children in a three-room house. He fixed up the house and made it feel like a mansion.

As he was losing his sons to war, he had to teach his daughters. He taught Goddie how to always look out for her younger siblings and how to pay attention to the details, never missing the nuances. Goddie always stared at his hands, which always looked ten years older than the rest of his body. The cracks were mean, and they rejected healing. He was still a masterpiece.

"Whatever the Lord geh yuh to do, do it well. Yuh 'ear me?" he said.

"Yes, Daadie, "she affirmed.

She could count on him to be honest with her, never going back and telling her secrets, forever listening and nodding. They looked out at the field. They never looked at each other. Goddie looked just like him. She was dark like him—sugar molasses like him. She smiled like him, and she was tall like him.

Goddie knew he liked her because he allowed her to size up to him. He saw himself in her and told her she would be the one who would rise. So, he took his time with her. He was never impatient. He was never rushed. He was always listening. Christopher Azariah Ormsby was his name, but Daadie was all Goddie needed.

"Mi bettah finish up di broomin and head to school," Goddie said.

"Yuh need anything, Daadie?"

"No, my dear. Gwaan ah school."

She pushed the dust off the veranda and leaned the brush broom to the side. After a moment inside, Goddie bounded down the porch and onto the path.

"Bye, Daadie," she yelled.

He gave a slight wave as she disappeared around the bend.

# CHAPTER 4

# WALKING HOME WITH JAMES

———

Afternoons in Spring Hill always seemed to be so busy. The children were busy catching up with friends. The taxis were busy shuttling parents and babies. The trucks were busy finishing the last of their deliveries. The road shops were busy capturing every sale, and even the street merchants were busy avoiding the end-of-day discounts.

Everyone was hurrying to finish their household chores before the sun set. Unlike the city lights of Kingston, darkness in the mountains meant just that, darkness. Anything after the late summer sunset was a fool's errand.

On any other day, Goddie would pick fruits along the way home and shed her school clothes as soon as she hit the gate. Even though they had goats to move, wood to split, kerosene to light, and bodies to bathe, she and her siblings would gather together and talk about the day. The afternoon was the greatest opportunity to simply be free. Free children. Free Jamaicans. Free Jamaica.

This particular afternoon was unusual for Goddie. She stayed back to get some help in math and review her recent homework assignment. Her classmate James Bailey decided to wait for her, as he lived just up the road from her gate. He was a quiet fellow but was no stranger to high grades and proper behavior.

James carried himself with a quiet strength. Goddie and her classmates only heard from him when he was uttering another correct answer to a question. To the class idiot, he was an annoyance, but for the rest, James represented the gold standard. He was the smartest one at school, and he made no apology. He did not smile often, but when he did, his smile was the sun.

His unassuming nature and polite stature reflected his good upbringing. His family was spread out all over the island, with many members in the United Kingdom. Goddie often watched in the yard as all the girls paid attention to him.

She had no interest in James or anyone else. It was all about school, school, and more school. She knew how hard Mumma scraped for school fees and allowing boys with white teeth to mess it up was not part of the plan. Undisciplined girls in the district always ended up breeding before time. She had no interest in unnecessary hardship.

Goddie sat in the classroom, waiting to talk to Mrs. Gabriel. From her desk, she could hear her classmates jumping into nearby Alcott Falls—a popular hangout spot for students before heading home from school. Like Goddie, everyone had evening chores, but they still found time to be teenagers. As hard as Jamaica was, it was still a tropical island. It was still a paradise, and for her friends, a dip in the water was a needed reprieve.

Goddie's failing grades in math meant she needed to stay back and get some help from Mrs. Gabriel. She knew her teacher could help. Mrs. Gabriel agreed to review Goddie's extra homework assignment and give her some guidance.

"Ok, Miss Ormsby, please review lesson fifteen and hand it in again," instructed Mrs. Gabriel. "You are a good student, but I don't hand out grades like candy. You will have to earn your graduation to the next level. I am willing to regrade your work if you can hand it in by Friday. Understand?"

Goddie listened intently as her teacher's voice carried from the front of the schoolhouse to the back and bounced off the floor. Mrs. Gabriel's eyebrows moved on her forehead like a conductor's wand. She did not suffer foolishness for long. She was misery personified, but she took a liking to Goddie.

Goddie always knew the condition of Mrs. Gabriel's shoes. That's all she saw as Mrs. Gabriel berated her academic sloppiness and laziness. She had left the comforts of nearby Annotto Bay to take the secondary teaching assignment in Spring Hill, and every day, Mrs. Gabriel let the world know what a mistake that was.

"Yes, ma'am," Goddie replied. She looked over her recent assignment with disappointment, as she knew her battles with math would wage on.

Goddie caught James looking at her, and she turned her paper to show him the C grade.

As the school yard emptied, Mrs. Gabriel shifted back into *patois*. While speaking the dialect was considered improper form, using the dialect connected better with her students. It was easier, and the headmaster was gone for the day. It was like she was slipping out of high heels and back into sandals phonetically.

"Yuh have one more opportunity tuh mek dis grade up before finals. I know yuh can raise it. Less complaining and more focus. I see James ah wait fi yuh. He can help yuh. Fi him grades need to be yuh grades," Mrs. Gabriel explained as she packed up.

Goddie shifted her eyes over to James. She was angry at the world, and right now, he was the world. She watched him wrinkle his brow in confusion as his election to math tutor was affirmed. She was better than her grades indicated. Academic excellence was more than a collection of capital letters.

She knew academic excellence was the only key to success. Jamaica's growing travel industry and heavy reliance on the agriculture areas meant the uneducated were relegated to either hotel labor, farm labor, or mining labor. Looking at that failing grade was just a reminder of what was waiting for her. Goddie wasn't interested.

James shifted his feet and slowly made his way to the door. He fussed with his school uniform but didn't say anything. Goddie wanted to unleash her anger on him, but he was now her only support. His very presence was a reminder of what she wasn't.

He leaned against the door frame and looked at the remaining students waiting for a ride home.

"Please close all di windows before yuh go home," requested Mrs. Gabriel.

Goddie was raging, but she knew who held the handle and who held the blade.

She sighed and said, "Yes, ma'am. James, come and help mi close dem shuttahs." James swung his body around and started on the first window. As they went from window to window, he wiped the tear falling down the side of his friend's face.

"Nuh worry 'bout it, Goddie. Mi wi help yuh wid di math homework. Buck up, mon," he said.

She looked over at him as she twisted the shutter latch and then moved to the last window. Acknowledging she needed help was a bitter pill and having the good-looking smart guy with the white teeth offer it didn't make it any easier. After what felt like a hundred windows, the two students ventured into the afternoon rush.

"Thanks fi waiting fi mi. Mi appreciate it very much," Goddie said.

"No problem."

It wasn't like Goddie needed an escort, but she was grateful for the chance to just talk and have company on the way home. It had rained most of the day, so the soppy schoolyard made for a slippery and miserable commute.

Any opportunity to distract from the remnants of the afternoon storm was welcomed as far as she was concerned. James offered to carry her books, but she wouldn't hear of it.

Daadie could see around corners, and she knew it. Whatever Daadie didn't see, her brothers, cousins, and church members would surely report on.

"Nevermind di math. How yuh do on deh English test? High grade, right?" James inquired.

She was one of the smart girls in the class, so he seized the opportunity to cheer her up. James walked a few yards and then turned. "Well?" he asked with eyebrows raised and white teeth shining.

She shifted her book weight and kept walking. She was still steaming about the math grade. She closed her eyes, and when she opened them, her long lashes flicked away the question.

He raised his eyebrows higher, and it seemed like for a second, his teeth got even whiter.

"James, yuh have plans after secondary school?" Goddie asked. She knew she wasn't answering his first question, but she didn't care.

The two friends became more reflective as they navigated the crumbling road. The August rains had softened up the hill, and the erosion crawled its way onto the road home. The walk home from school now became a negotiation between slogging in mud, falling in the gulley, or hanging on to each other. The last option wouldn't happen, perhaps much to James's disappointment.

"Mi father wants to send mi away fi school," he said, sighing.

Goddie looked over at James, "Whut mek yuh sound sad? Yuh nuh wan to get outta here? Jamaica nice but dis yah life hard. Time tuh look fi more."

"Well, I don't know 'bout dat. Mi father sending mi tuh live wid his sistah inna London," he lamented.

"Well then, mi wi guh a London an yuh help get mi sistahs ready fi school den." Goddie chortled.

They kept walking up the hill toward the post office when the postman sped by them and stopped ahead. He hopped out of the truck and began to sort the envelopes, packages, and barrel notices from foreign countries.

His uniform was wet, and his wide brim hat offered no solace from the afternoon rain. As they walked past the truck, they couldn't help but notice the envelopes from the United Kingdom.

Letters from anywhere always looked different. The red and blue stripes were the dead give away and with that, there was always excitement to see what loved ones were doing abroad.

Goddie didn't have all the details, but she knew there had to be more outside of Jamaica.

It was an internal battle and a careful subject, as desires to leave were seen as abandonment and desires to stay felt like betrayal of the soul.

Jamaica was changing, and those who wanted to reach their potential were wise to recognize what an opening looked like. Opportunities to pursue studies outside Jamaica were not automatically given. Class and status trumped blackness, and money always swung the door open. Opportunities in Jamaica were like doors. If some had wide-open doors, then others just had the door slightly cracked. Goddie would either crawl under the door or create a door herself. Nothing would be handed to her.

"Goddie, dis a yuh gate, right?" said James.

Goddie leaned on the post and looked at James. "Yeah... yuh should guh to London James. Foreign is callin' yuh. Yuh not going jus' fe yuh. Yuh going fi all a wi," she despaired.

He adjusted the weight of his book bag and gave her a smile before heading up the road.

James looked back and waved. "Inna di morrows, Goddie. Nuh worry yuhself bout it."

"Lickkle more, James."

Goddie watched him for a bit. It wasn't because he was a nice guy. He was the only one who acknowledged her. James was her only intellectual equal.

For as far as she could see him, she wanted to switch places. It was selfish, but her future required it. Selfishness was the grease that would squeeze her through. She knew she would be ready when the day came.

As he turned the corner at Shantimy Road, she shifted her weight off the post and headed up the path to the house. She walked slowly up the path, her feet absorbing every deviation and abrasion. She wasn't in a hurry. Four siblings were waiting for her, and now, so was her math book.

# PART II

# POTS
# AND PAINS

## CHAPTER 5

# MUMMA

---

The treachery of navigating the soaked path along the precipice of Blue Mountain was only for the drunken or foolish. The B1 road in Portland was a secondary road that stretched across both St. Andrew and Portland parish. It started in Papine, St. Andrew, and wound its way north through the Blue Mountain range to Spring Hill and beyond.

Eventually, after carving its path through Gordon Town, it came to rest thirty-two miles later on the north shore town of Buff Bay. Calling this artery anything other than a hardened path would be an insult to both carts and vehicles alike.

The canopy overhead hid the lies the road kept as many a cart lost its wheel on the broken-down road. Worn divots in the mountain provided safe harbor to cars passing on the left, and grace and mercy covered those on the right.

Anyone willing to risk the fourth gear on B1 was soon corrected by hairpin turns without guardrails. The August rain made passing a fool's errand, and the gully was ready to receive its next guest at any time. For Spring Hill residents, B1 was a lifeline. It was the only road to Kingston and the markets.

Homes in the district suffered badly engineered and unstable infrastructure. The roads were easily washed out with the August rains, preventing harvested goods from reaching the market. The main roads would at least allow for goods and services to travel reasonably to the country. Without the main roads, farmers would not generate income.

The government maintained the B1 death trap while local parochial and unclassified roads were preserved by the parish. Most families lived off the good highway, up higher in the hills. Farms took advantage of the mountain slopes and built their fields there. Houses were hard to see from B1, but they were there. Goddie lived with her family tucked back from the road, with only the odd gate post to mark the entry. Finding the house either required a good eye or good nose, as Mumma's cooking never failed to lead her home.

As Goddie walked up the path home, she saw in the distance Mumma cooking away. She could see the smoke rising on the backside of the house, which faced the road. Goddie sensed something was wrong. As she ventured closer, Mumma was hunched over a pot, stirring and looking around. Her frustration thickened the closer Goddie got to the house. Flung pots and country swear words failed to explain the problem.

"Rhaatid," Mumma muttered.

Goddie didn't need to be close to know why Mumma was cussing. She had run out of flour, and she never ever runs out of flour. Mumma checked the bag, checked another bag, and finally reached for a tin. There was just dust in the tin. Next, she checked for cornmeal. Nothing.

Her frustration was palpable and scalding. Mumma knew she had to feed her family, manage the house, and care for the babies. Having flour in supply was a basic responsibility.

Goddie noticed Mumma was tired. Labor couldn't care less about the laborer. As Goddie studied her mother, she apologized in her mind without being charged with anything. With all the confusion and frustration, Mumma homed in on her middle child watching from the turn.

"LAURETTA!" she shouted. Standing there with hands on hip and jaw tightening, she whipped her gaze to the turn. "Wuh yuh hiding from? Weh yuh sistah?" Mumma asked.

Goddie froze. No answer seemed like the only answer.

Mumma's jaw tightened another notch, and she went in again. "LAURETTA! BERT! Mumma shouted again........ silence.

Lambert and Lauretta were nowhere to be found. The goats offered up a retort. The ox tied to the gate swung its head to the left but offered no solace. The fuse was lit, and the combustion of exhaustion and a setting sun finally released on the middle child.

"Mi jus arrived from skool. Mi nuh know," explained Goddie.

Yuh betta know. Guh fine her, please."

"Yes, ma'am." Goddie dropped her books and took off around the other side of the house, looking to find what she knew she would not find, while Mumma tried to figure out how to save dinner with a boiling pot and not enough flour.

She scoured the house and closest field only to come back with the next best alternative...Amoziah. Everyone called him Vurley, but if an older sister didn't work, an older brother was still one layer of protection from the belt.

"Yes, Mumma?" Vurley wondered.

"Guh ova tuh Miss Eileen an aks Michelle fi two-pound ah flour fi mi, please. Nuh flour, Nuh supper," Mumma explained.

Vurley put his hands on his hips and stepped closer to their mother. "Why yuh never send Goddie tuh get di flour? She was standing right yah suh when yuh did call mi."

Mumma looked up from the pot, and Vurley realized this exchange wouldn't end well. He disappeared around the corner toward Miss Eileen. As the fire blazed, Mumma removed the pot from the heat to wait for the flour.

As Goddie studied her mother, Mumma's frustration felt deeper. She checked the fire and drifted toward the back step. Her eyes scanned the area without resting on anyone. Unsure what was happening, Goddie inched closer.

Mumma dragged a basket of yams toward her. She pulled another knife off the ledge and handed it to Goddie. She never let Goddie handle the sharp knife, so Goddie listened carefully. Goddie searched the basket for the yam that would make her look like a chef. She gripped the vegetable in one hand and her trusted weapon in the other.

"Follow me and don't cut yuh fingah," Mumma instructed. Whatever she was about to say must have been important because all of the *patois* went away, and her voice became like the king's English.

She carved a notch in the yam and handed it to her. Goddie watched for a minute and then started in.

"Dis a ah hard life, Goddie. It tek more than it gives, and it costs more than it earns. Slavery is ova but slave work neva ends. My girl, mi nuh know wah God has in store. Buh when you see it, yuh better run for it. Don't mek it pass yuh," lectured Mumma.

A strange silence entered. Only the boiling pot spoke.

Mumma, fixated on the yams, explained further. "I wanted tuh finish mi education. Mi did tink maybe I wud become ah shop keeper or nurse. Some from di district left for foreign. Dem neva did cum bac. I wanted to be wid dem. Yuh pupa was very nice suh mi stayed wid him. He took care of me."

"Yes, ma'am," acknowledged Goddie.

Caroline was Mumma's given name. Goddie knew when Caroline spoke English, she needed to listen. Mumma was Mumma, but Caroline was the queen.

Mumma dropped the knife and grabbed both sides of Goddie's face. She looked deep into her eyes. Goddie could smell her. She could see the breakfast still in her teeth. Goddie had never seen all the wrinkles up close before. She studied everything. Her eyelashes that once waved now just functioned.

Goddie gazed into Caroline's eyes. *Who was this sad person?* She could see the gray hair grain peeking under Mumma's wrap and felt her hands pressed into her face like a wrench.

The fifty years had dimmed Mumma's eyes, but Goddie could see past that. Life had carved its worth on Caroline with no reward. All the coconut oil in the world couldn't hide the truth.

"Yuh a di middle pickney buh yuh 'ave di best hope. Yuh sistah Lauretta not showing mi anyting. Yuh must rise now. It is important yuh stand on yuh own. A husband is good, buh yuh must be able tuh carry yuh own. Study yuh books. Nuh mek these bwoys dem confuse yuh. Give yuhself as much chance as possible," Caroline preached.

Mumma had said more to her in two minutes than she muttered in two weeks. It was all quite strange and quite preparatory.

"Yuh 'ear me? When di window opens fah yuh, fly through," she whispered as the patois reassumed its position.

As the gravel announced Vurley's return, Mumma released Goddie, and just like that, the transmission was broken.

"Miss Eileen sen ova three-pound ah flour. She seh don't worry bout it," Vurley exclaimed. He placed the flour on the ground near Goddie and stared at both of them.

"Anything else?" questioned Vurley.

"Guh help yuh pupa move di goats tuh di other side. Goddie finish di yams," Mumma replied.

Vurley was gone before Mumma could turn her attention back to him.

As Goddie started in on the yams, her eyes studied Mumma.

Mumma stared into the pot, and the sadness stared back. She lifted her head to the field. Goddie knew there was more to Mumma than just harvesting, cooking, cleaning, and nursing. The quiet between them was solemn. The scrape of the pot kept time in the silence.

"Are yuh happy?" Goddie asked.

Mumma left the pot and sat beside her daughter. She grabbed her hand and looked out.

"What is happiness?" Mumma questioned.

As they sat and looked out, Goddie could feel Mumma's grip become firmer, and a strange feeling came over Goddie. Mumma was beginning the transfer. Every vision, every detail, every dream, every hope, and every wish was being supplanted deep inside Goddie. All of this felt quite strange but quite sure. Boiling soup bubbled audibly, breaking the silence between them.

"Yuh pupa has bin very good tuh mi. But he's getting older an will soon becum ah pickney again. Mi nuh waah nuh more pickney," she lamented. "Mi waah fi mi time now." Her chief complaint was interrupted by the sound of boiling soup and the men coming toward the house as the day ended.

As she bent over to finish the supper, Goddie saw Mumma as a whole woman. Her hands were worn but resistant even to the highest heat. The rhythm of cutting yams gave license not just to stare at Mumma but at Caroline, the woman.

In that moment, Goddie knew Caroline had done the best with what she had. Her clothing was simple. She wore the same dress every day. The one with puffy shoulders, long sleeves, billowing skirt, and flowing undergarments. She was always dressed up with nowhere to go. Her garments were patterned with the dirt of the garden and the grease of the fire. She carried herself with regalness.

She was more than just a mother. She was the standard bearer of queens. She was the cross beam of the household. It all stood or fell with her. She knew it. She was resigned to it. Spring Hill had taken the best of her.

# CHAPTER 6

# POTS AND PAINS

---

"Julie! ...... JULIE!" Goddie shouted. The family rarely used birth names when speaking, but Minnette deserved every ounce of it.

She and her three siblings had been sleeping bunched up and perpendicular on a queen bed for years. When it was time for bed, everyone faced the same direction. By morning, Minnette always ended up in positions she hadn't gone to bed in.

It was the same formula every night and the same harassment every morning. The snoring, of course, was the pièce de ré·sis·tance. One would have thought that Lambert and Daadie were cutting boards outside except for the fact the rumble wasn't but a foot away.

So, with Minnette's feet now two inches away from Goddie's face, she returned her disgusted gaze to the slice of daylight coming through the aluminum roof. The daydream was sweet, but this rusty foot child mashed up the moment. She tried again to return to the daydream, but the smell was too much.

"What is it? Can't yuh si mi sleeping? I'm telling Mumma yuh wake me for no reason," said Minnette.

"Ah, good. Go tell her. At least you will be outta dis bed. Tell her about yuh rusty feet and snoring too," replied Goddie.

Minnette kissed her teeth, flung the sheet off her, and marched out the room.

Goddie couldn't care less. The peace of the moment was worth the price of the war later.

With rest vanquished, the district awake, and the sun overseeing it all, Goddie hopped off the bed and decided to join the Ormsby society. Not wanting to be drafted into heavy duty, she calculated her footsteps through the empty house to the back window. As she got closer, she heard Mumma arguing with Lauretta in the outside kitchen. Goddie leaned on the open window and eavesdropped.

"Ah, time yuh start to think 'bout your future girl. Running around wid di friends dem nah cut it wid yuh father. What is the plan?"

Goddie watched from the window as Lauretta was visibly getting more and more upset.

"Mumma, I just want to make dumplings in peace without interrogation," pleaded Lauretta.

"Well?" Mumma asked, ignoring Lauretta's request.

"Mumma, I'm not sure what I want to pursue. I want to do nursing, but how I'm suppose tuh go? Money tight," Lauretta explained.

Mumma stopped cooking and turned around. "The only ting tight is yuh skirt, my dear. It's about desire and determination, not dancing and skylarking, mi dear. If yuh spent as much time studying as yuh do eating shrimp at di river, yuh wud be in London now. It's not yuh dreams yuh carrying. It's mine," Mumma explained.

Mumma threw down the knife and went over to stoke the fire. There was to be no discussion with Mumma.

"Studying yuh books is the only alternative to this life," Mumma explained as she came back to the table and resumed cutting the vegetables for the curry chicken. "Yuh do not want dis life, Lauretta. Dis is not life. Yuh must set yuh sights on higher heights, my dear."

"But I…"

"SHUT yuh mout." Mumma raised her hand. Lauretta stepped back and got quiet. They cooked the remainder of the meal in silence. Goddie took in the exchange as she watched through the window. Inside was safer, and she knew it.

Her younger sister Dearis came bounding through the door with all the noise in the world. Delphina was her given name, but she only heard that out loud when she was in trouble.

"Who Mumma vex with?" asked Dearis. The slamming door swung Goddie's head away from the open window and stopped Dearis in her tracks.

"Shut yuh mout. Mumma fighting with Lauretta and me ah watch. Either hush yuh mout or go," snapped Goddie. She could feel Dearis' face pressed against her skirt. She looked under her arm to see her sister's pitiful eyes and wrapped her arm around her.

"Ok, come look and see," Goddie said as she pulled her sister close.

"Not a word. If yuh mess up my spot, it's big trouble fi yuh," warned Goddie.

"Ok…" Dearis whispered, wiping away the beginnings of tears.

Goddie didn't often get to look around. There was always something to do. Always something to cut. Always something to wipe. Her mother and sister couldn't see her in the window, so she soaked in the exclusive spying session.

Goddie watched as Mumma used pimento wood to give the food a smoky taste. She marveled as Mumma made feasts out of next to nothing. Kitchen was perhaps too fancy a word. What Mumma had was surely not fancy.

Goddie remembered her brother calling the kitchen area a kreng kreng. It really wasn't much. It was just an outside cooking area made up of some rocks with firewood underneath. She noted how the bigger rocks would support the larger pots for boiling and purification. The refrigeration was nothing more than the ability to cure meat over the open fire. The smoke from cooking would cure the meat, and Mumma would salt it for storage.

Curing the meat was critical to ensure that the family had enough to survive during the low months. Lauretta was in charge of the salt and pimento grain that would seal the meat. In most cases, the meat would just hang there, and when the family was ready for it, they would take off a piece of it and cook it.

Goddie shifted her gaze from the window to Dearis. She realized, just as Mumma was guiding Lauretta, she would be responsible for setting the example for her sister and younger siblings. Mumma couldn't do it all, and Goddie knew she had to get it right.

Whether it was cornmeal, porridge, or her famous rundown breakfast, Goddie had to learn how to cook all the meals and seal them in her memory. The tense silence between Lauretta and Mumma meant Goddie could go unnoticed. Studying the cooking session seemed more important than the weekend math homework waiting for her.

"Clean out the pot stove and sharpen the knife," Mumma commanded.

"Yes, ma'am," replied Lauretta.

Lauretta took the small knife and, with the sharpening stick, sharpened it up to perfection. As she split the chicken pieces into parts, she looked up to catch Goddie staring out the window. Their eyes met and locked for an eternity. Goddie sensed the sadness and turned away. She wanted to help, but she didn't want the price that came with it. Mumma's wrath wasn't worth the lesson.

"Hurry up, mon. The fire getting hot," complained Mumma.

"Yes, ma'am."

Lauretta cut the chicken with accuracy to ensure everyone got their fair share without fighting. She dropped some of the pieces into the pot of water and positioned all the vegetables on a wood plank for cooking.

One by one, she quartered and split each vegetable. First the carrots, then the potatoes. Then she skinned the garlic quarters and cut them into small pieces. There was no exam on this lesson, but the consequences of forgetting weighed heavily on Goddie's mind.

"Bring me the scotch bonnet, Lauretta," Mumma asked.

Her irritation level was subsiding. Goddie didn't care. She wasn't going out there, and technically she was babysitting Dearis.

Lauretta added the scotch bonnet pepper in small doses and then added in more chicken pieces.

"Anything else, ma'am?" Lauretta beseeched as she stared at Goddie hanging out the window.

"Yes, nuh badda try and run weh. Yuh can run wid yuh friends dem latah. Time tuh learn something," warned Mumma.

Lauretta sighed as she added the remaining pieces of chicken into the simmering pot and stirred it around quickly. With the remaining seasoning, Mumma poured them over the cooking pieces to bring out the succulent smells and taste. Who knew anger could smell so good? Mumma added water and covered the pot to stew.

Goddie, now with Dearis peeking through the open window, took in the lesson. Beyond the disappointment of Lauretta and the irritation of Mumma, watching her sister and mother cooking was sacred to Goddie. It reminded her she had so much to learn.

Mumma turned to start the saltfish breakfast on the next pot and suddenly stopped.

"Yuh can stop hiding now, Goddie. Food can't cook itself. Bring yuh sistah and come learn something," commanded Mumma.

Dearis looked up at Goddie as she pressed her lips together. The spy game was over.

"I'm waiting on yuh. Let's go," Mumma commanded.

Goddie opened the back door and her nostrils filled with the scents of ackee, tomatoes, and bell peppers. She grabbed a bowl of yams and began to peel.

"Goddie, you and Lauretta are heading into womanhood now. Di time fi friends and rampin must stop. Focus an' hard work must begin. Yuh pupa an' I nuh want dis life fi yuh. Workin' dis farm a hard life. Dream biggah than this place. Learn di tings yuh need and build yuh life," lectured Mumma.

The sound of the wood spoon scraping the pot was all that could be heard. Goddie looked at Lauretta, and Dearis looked at Mumma. The class was in session, and there would be no repeat. Goddie sensed she wouldn't be giving this message much longer. As she delivered the word, her English became clearer. She wanted every word to be heard.

Mumma stirred and lectured, "I demand more from you because I see more in you. Hold up di womanhood of Jamaica.

Tek what I could not and go where I could not. Time is not to be wasted. Be ready for the opportunity and run through the door. Don't walk. Run. Run, I say.......Run."

Lauretta and Dearis looked on as Mumma addressed Goddie.

Mumma turned away from her girls. They could see she was wiping her eyes and nose. She wanted to be heard, and she was.

The silence was heavy. The only sound was the spoon scraping the bottom of the Dutch pot.

Goddie and Lauretta looked at each other. The rest of the meal was cooked in silence.

# CHAPTER 7

# BUN UP PLANTAIN

———

Goddie took the plantain off the shelf and sharpened the knife. She felt the moisture of the wood and assembled the fire as Daadie showed her. The fire caught quickly, and she set the pan steady on the grate. It would be her first time cooking on her own, but she had to learn. As she waited for the pan to heat, she organized the ingredients.

The first plantain cut fairly evenly, but the second one was too ripe and didn't hold up well under the knife. Whatever the knife lacked, Goddie made up in determination. Mumma deserved a good breakfast, and she would make it happen. Goddie took out some flour, salt, and cooking oil. Dumpling time. She had only watched Mumma do it a few times and Lauretta once.

She exhaled and began the process. She dumped the flour out and added water. As she kneaded the flour, she kept one eye on the plantain cooking. Burning the food wasn't an option.

*Pay attention, Goddie,* she mentored herself. *Watch the edges and flip. Watch the edges and flip. Watch the edg...*"

"Weh yuh ah duh?" interrupted Lauretta. She burst out in laughter at the thought of Goddie cooking anything edible. She brushed up against Goddie and looked over her shoulder.

"Shh... I'm surprising Mumma. Shut yuh mout," warned Goddie.

Lauretta laughed, "If yuh burn up Mumma kitchen, she will bust yuh batty. That will match yuh burning plantains over there."

Goddie turned to see the black smoke rising from what was once sweet plantain. Lauretta, unable to contain her joy, hollered all the way around the corner.

Goddie removed the charred remnants from the pot and began to cry. She wanted it to be perfect, but it was far from it.

As she continued kneading the dough, she caught the shadow out the corner of her eye. Daadie and Mumma were watching her from the window with the biggest smiles.

"Add more wood to di fire," Daadie instructed from the open window. Mumma made her way outside and stood there with arms crossed.

"Need help?" Mumma asked.

"Yes, ma'am. Not much of a surprise. Sorry, Mumma."

Mumma wrapped her arms around Goddie, wiped her tears, and placed her hands on her face.

"Mi would rather yuh try and fail than never try at all. I spent a lot of time afraid tuh try. Never be afraid tuh try. Hear me?" She squeezed her middle child tight and started finishing off the breakfast with her. Mumma added salt to the dough and beat it into submission.

Goddie tried to figure out the best way to help Mumma without getting in the way. She watched how gently Mumma placed the dumpling balls in the oil. She was careful not to splash the oil. Goddie couldn't help but notice the sadness return to Mumma's face.

"You ok?" Goddie inquired. "You're not vex wid me about burning the plantain, are you?"

Mumma smiled and looked at her.

"Nuh, I'm not vex." After a long pause, she looked back at Goddie.

Goddie watched as a heaviness came over Mumma and Daadie. Their movements slowed down, and all expression left their face. At first, Goddie thought they were tired, but they had just gotten up. Something was wrong. She had never seen Daadie so silent.

"Yuh were number five, but yuh did suppose to be number six," Mumma whispered as she rescued the plantain.

"What yuh mean, Mumma?"

"Mi did have a baby, but it didn't survive. Today was the day," explained Mumma.

They both stood there in silence, cooking Goddie's surprise breakfast. Daadie leaned out the window, listening. His eyes met the floor and never moved the whole time.

"Sumtimes in life, things nuh go how yuh expect. Yuh have to keep moving forward. Neva stop, Goddie. Yuh stop, yuh die too," said Mumma.

Goddie stared at the ground, but by this time, Minnette and Lassie were standing on the stoop. Goddie had the feeling no one else knew Mumma's secret. She decided to keep it that way. Besides, her sisters were too young to accept such strange information.

"Why all the sadness? Wah Goddie do?" piped in Minnette.

Goddie could see Minnette salivating at the chance to get her in trouble.

Goddie watched as Lassie looked between all the adults and shifted her head from side to side. Her missing teeth validated her standing as the baby. She stood at the door with remnants of a straw doll and the blanket she dragged everywhere.

"Nothing," Mumma answered. "Goddie made us a feast breakfast by herself. Guh wash yuh hands and come eat."

As Goddie washed up, she studied her hands. She had the same hands as Mumma and stood almost as tall as Daadie. As the water ran through her fingers, she resolved she could do anything, just like her Mumma and Daadie.

Goddie wondered about her missing sibling. She didn't wonder long because she knew God was in everything, including the things she didn't understand.

"Dis breakfast is good, Goddie!" said Lassie between bites and swallows.

"Thanks."

Goddie looked over a Mumma. She was smiling again.

## CHAPTER 8

# CHICKENS, BULLET HOLES, AND MACHETES

———

Catching one chicken was a fool's game. Trying to catch three chickens was an exercise in futility. Goddie had made it her mission to outsmart these hens.

"Rass.....blasted fowl," cussed Goddie.

"Come nuh? When I catch you, it's dinner fe yuh," she warned. She had spent the last hour trying to gather up the chickens before the afternoon storm came through Spring Hill.

"Why me, Lord?" Goddie asked between gasps as she chased the third and final chicken off the porch, down the path, and around the house. The first two figured out the jig was up, but this one was not going down so easy. Freedom is a taste not easily forgotten…especially for a chicken. Around the house she went again, back under the ox cart and over the porch.

"Yuh gonna meet dat pot for sure tonight," gasped Goddie.

She rasped as she stopped to let her lungs catch up with her heart. The chicken stopped too. The game was exhausting, and both parties acknowledged it. Goddie studied the gathering clouds, and the chicken watched her. The August rainy season had not relented, and today was no exception. The sky would open up any minute now.

Just when round four was about to begin, a full-bodied silhouette darkened the veranda door.

"Yuh waitin' upon duh Lord's return?" asked Daadie. "Catch di fowl an' tell Lincoln to come in now. The rain is coming, and he's been beating up sugar cane fuh hours. The cane must be dead now tuh rhaatid." Daadie only cussed when he was frustrated.

"Lincoln is here? In Spring Hill? I thought he was in Kingston fi more training," Goddie said.

She tried to hold back her excitement, as Daadie clearly wasn't in the mood. She brushed off the dust from the front of her dress and kept the corners of her mouth from curling up in glee.

Lincoln was her favorite sibling. He was born a few years before Goddie, and she had always looked up to him. Goddie's nickname for Lincoln was Doctah. He didn't like the name at first, but it grew on him. He didn't come to Spring Hill much after returning from the war. Daadie said Lincoln preferred to spend time in Kingston to look for work and meet up with returning soldiers. Goddie welcomed this news as a gift.

Daadie's glare broke Goddie's daydream. "Eh gyal. Stop gazing. Go out and git him."

"Yes, sir," Goddie replied and turned to her feathered nemesis. "Today fuh yuh. Tomorrow fe me. Daadie saved you today," Goddie whispered to the chicken, and with that, she walked around the house toward the open field.

The chicken watched her go around the corner, tilted its head to be sure, and made its way down the path to rejoin the other feathered brethren.

Goddie put a pep in her step and hurried along. She brushed the remnant dirt particles and feathers from her dress and perfected her posture.

As she made her way through the field, she could hear the whack of the machete come into chorus with the exhaust of Lincoln's voice.

He swung the machete with malice. The cane was shown no mercy. The cadence of his swing was ominous. The cane knew better than to put up a fight. *Why was he so upset?* Goddie wondered to herself. It was strange to see him in the field so late, as harvesting normally started in the morning hours. It was even stranger to see him create all this cleanup work knowing the storm clouds were gathering.

Whatever it was, Goddie would take her chances on his mood. Afterall, it was her brother Doctah, and she was glad to see him.

She hadn't seen Lincoln in two years as he had enlisted in the military. He was serving under the British Army stationed in Europe. As she walked up closer to him, her admiration of her brother increased with each step. He was tall and long, but he was strong.

His blackness didn't hide the scars on his back. His time in Germany was relentless. He had seen his share of battles and training exercises. He had withstood the very worst that the British Army and American segregation could give him.

Goddie heard he had been shot in the shoulder, but she wouldn't dare bring it up.

As she got closer, she started to notice how much he resembled Daadie. He wasn't the oldest brother, but he was the strongest brother. He wasn't very loud or very commanding, but his presence was honest.

He had seen a lot of things, and not everything one sees can be spoken of. Goddie understood that some things had to be kept inside one's chest to keep the body warm. His face resembled Mumma, but the rest of him belonged to Christopher Ormsby. His back was the same. His neck was the same. His legs were the same. Everything was the same. Same. Same. Same. Everything about him screamed Daadie. *Why wouldn't it? Heroes always begat heroes,* she thought.

"Hey," Goddie yelled as she waved.

Lincoln turned his head and lit up. He dropped the machete and waved Goddie over. He was still a few yards away, but for some reason, she could still see all thirty-six of his teeth smiling. She picked up the pace and waved back.

It felt good to be welcomed by her big brother. Goddie liked how he made her feel more grown than she was. She felt like his equal, and she was proud of that.

"Whuh a gwaan? Everyting gud?" Lincoln questioned. He took a moment to look her over as if he was checking for damage. Goddie knew he loved her and took every opportunity to protect her. After the inspection, the smile poked out briefly.

"Everything is everything. Daadie sey to come in now. How yuh going to gather all dis yah sugar cane?" she questioned, looking around.

"That's why Daadie sent you. Come on." Lincoln laughed.

The two siblings began to pile the stalks together. Lincoln did the piling, and Goddie bound the piles together. As they worked, she took note of her hero.

Lincoln's exuberance somehow faded, and Goddie noticed melancholy setting in with each pile of cane. The gathering storm clouds echoed his disposition as the storm held back its strength. The distance rumble and increasing wind stood in agreement with him.

"Yuh luk even taller now. How di grades?" he asked. As the words left his lips, the thunder started to give notice.

Goddie looked at the ground and explained. "Math ah give problem but everything is good. Looking forward to finishing soon." The thunder filled in the awkward silence. She felt bad about struggling in school.

Lincoln smirked and put his arm around his sister. "It's alright, mon. I'm not di one yuh have to explain tuh. That job is for Daadie. Come, let's clean up."

As Lincoln gathered and Goddie bundled, they chatted. Goddie shared her troubles at school, and Lincoln talked about his time in the war. The more he talked, the more she understood her brother on a deeper level. Lincoln had his own mind. He felt that leaving Jamaica and joining the war effort was his opportunity to defend king and country.

Goddie couldn't help but think it was his opportunity to get out of Jamaica. But somehow, through the process of the war, he had changed. She determined no one ever really knows what happens to a man once he leaves his home and joins the front line.

The two worked fast against the coming storm. Piling and binding. Piling and binding. The storm had run out of patience and was advancing. It would be nasty.

Goddie took her dress and wiped the sweat. As she bundled the last pile of cane, she stood up. "Cyan I ask you a question?"

Lincoln took one of the cane pieces and peeled back a strip with his teeth. "What duh yuh want tuh know?"

"Why yuh come back to Jamaica? Why yuh nevah stay in London?" Her eyes ran from his boots on past his belt to meet his face. Goddie wanted to hear from her brother.

Lincoln's countenance changed. Before he answered, he assessed the storm clouds and took out a sharpening stone. Lincoln then began to rub along the edge of the machete slowly. With each stroke, she noticed the blade getting sharper and sharper. He tested the blade with a whisper of grass, and the blade didn't disappoint. She watched as he sharpened from the tip to the base; every inch of the blade gained his meticulous attention.

His jaw tightened and his eyes narrowed. When he exhaled this time, his nose flared, and his eyes traveled from the ground to meet Goddie.

""I was tired of deh boy talk. Boy dis. Boy dat. Tired of it." he explained.

"The damn Yankee bwoy dem think they can talk to black people any kind of way. Not me. Nevah. The war made me an angry person. England made me an angry person. We can die for England but can't work for England. Dem nah give out jobs to blacks. Only the females dem get work. The only ting the war gave me was a bullet in the shoulder, pain forever, and no sleep," said Lincoln.

He cut the conversation short and put away the machete. Goddie resolved that despite his pet name, Doctah was the one in need of the most healing.

With mercy, the rain started falling. It may as well. Lincoln didn't have any more tears to give. He left the island a strong Jamaican and was suddenly entangled with American whites, American blacks, British whites, and Europeans. His disillusionment was palpable. Goddie gathered up the last of the cane.

She felt bad for her older brother. The war had not been kind to him, and she sensed he wasn't happy to be home. *What really happened to him? What did he see?* she wondered.

Lincoln relented. "Come on, Goddie, let's go. It's getting bad now." He picked up the machete and grabbed Goddie's arm.

They plowed their way through the torrential rain to the house. The wind blew the deluge sideways, and they could barely see the roof, let alone the house. Soaked to the bone, they held hands for the final few steps before the veranda.

Before going up the step, Lincoln grabbed Goddie by the shoulders and said, "Better study yuh book. Jamaica is hard life an' yuh can do bettah. Nuh worry yuhself 'bout Mumma and Daadie. When di time come, yuh will know. Don't mek Jamaica trap yuh. Never be afraid. Just go and start again."

Goddie looked up at Lincoln with tears forming in her eyes. He looked like Mumma. He was sad like Mumma. He was broken like Mumma. The rain didn't blur the frown in his eyes.

Goddie wished she could take some of his sadness, but her back wasn't broad enough. It was too heavy. As she wrapped her arms around his shoulders, she felt the scar from the bullet wound.

She traced the rim of the wound with her finger and wondered if the hole led to his heart. She had never loved him more. As she looked over his shoulder, she could see Daadie coming through the veranda door with a plate in one hand and a bottle torch in the other.

"You two wet chickens come inside now. Lightning is falling," Daadie insisted.

Goddie held Lincoln's hand tight, and together they left the storm to its devices.

## CHAPTER 9

# GREEN BANANA PORRIDGE

——

Goddie had been studying her math for a few weeks. She was getting better, but she needed more practice. It was the weekend, and she wanted a quick breakfast before beginning her morning study session.

She managed to slither through three sleeping bodies and start a fire outside. She had already gathered and chopped the green bananas. The milk stood ready, and the nutmeg, cinnamon, and sugar awaited instructions. She put on Mumma's apron.

All she needed was the small pot. She searched all around the outdoor kitchen area. Nothing. She stacked the small Dutch pots into bigger Dutch pots. She moved everything in the outside kitchen. Like an escaped prisoner, the burnt pot revealed itself. She figured someone must have burnt some food in the pot and hid it. *Nice*, thought Goddie.

She whispered, "I'm so glad dis neva me," as she put some water in the pot and set it on the fire. Maybe she could heat it up and clean it out without anyone noticing. Daadie would be upset to know someone burned up Mumma's pot. Things were tight on the farm, so creating more expense put pressure on him.

"Everyting alright?" said a familiar voice through the back window. "Whuh yuh burning up out there?" Daadie asked.

Goddie sighed as she watched the idea of studying early slowly slip away. Instead of a quick breakfast, she worried she would have to answer Daadie's questions about a pot she had nothing to do with. She knew she would never pass the upcoming math test without more studying.

"Whoever left this pot to burn up now has me starting my breakfast all ova again. I was doing jus' fine until dis," Goddie explained as she avoided eye contact with Daadie and scrubbed the inside of the pot.

Goddie felt bad about waking up Daadie. He worked twelve hours a day, and this was his one day to rest. She scrubbed as hard as she could down the walls of the pot, switching hands every few strokes to keep up the momentum. She figured the faster she scrubbed, the faster he could go back to sleep.

As the burnt pot continued to torment her, she looked up again and he was gone. She stopped mid-stroke and looked around. It was still dark, so he could come from anywhere. Fearing a belt, she panicked as she scraped the black bottom and carved the burned sides until aluminum made its appearance. The more she scraped, the more the aluminum showed up for work.

Without breaking stride, she noticed the sun hadn't risen yet. Even the sun didn't want any part of this. "Dis rhaatid pot," Goddie cussed.

With the fire still on duty, the ingredients waiting, and the sun checking to see if it was safe, Goddie gave all she could to the relentless crucible. Out of the morning darkness, a hand reached out and grabbed her arm. As she turned her head, the wrinkles on his fingers and muscles in his palms were all she needed. Daadie had returned and the reckoning came with him.

"Stop now. I think the pot is sorry," he said, chuckling.

Goddie ran her eyes from his fingers down his forearm up over his shoulder to meet his eyes. His missing teeth didn't dampen the amusement he was getting at his daughter's expense. She couldn't see his other hand, so she braced for the worst. He released her arm and grabbed the pot handle.

Goddie withdrew her sore hands from inside the pot and waited for the judgment. She closed her eyes. The silence was forever. She peered through the slit in her eyes, and there it was.

A new pot.

Daadie consoled her. "Sumtime yuh have to forgive yourself an' start ova. It's ok tuh start ova' sumtime. Everyting nuh always go as planned. What yuh plan for ah nuh what God plan for. Sumtime he have ah betta plan. Dis is your betta plan," he said as he held up a shiny new pot. He nudged her out the way and started putting the ingredients together.

"Here, tek your frustration out on this," he said as he handed her more green bananas to peel.

She stood beside him and used her thumb to start the peel. He heated up the milk over the fire and added the mashed bananas one at a time. He handed her the nutmeg and cinnamon stick to grate as he stirred. The porridge was finally coming together.

She looked over at her father as he continued stirring.

"It's ok to start again, Goddie," he smirked as he stirred without turning his head. "This won't be the first time or the last time things don't go the way yuh want. Always remember yuh can start again. You can change your mind. Just decide and go. Understand?"

"Yes, sir," she replied, grating the nutmeg over Daadie's creation. He stretched his arm around her and gave her a squeeze. She knew when he was trying to advise her. His *patois* took a back seat to the King's English.

"So why were you up so early? asked Daadie.

"I wanted to study for my math exam coming up. Math a give me big trouble," Goddie said.

He nodded and stirred as she kept talking.

Goddie continued, "If I can get a high mark on the next test, I won't fail the class."

Daadie continued to nod and stir.

"I just want to give myself the best chance after school is over," she explained.

Daadie continued to nod and stir. Then he looked up and forward without breaking the stirring. He brushed the rest of the nutmeg into the pot and mixed it in. "Bring yuh bowl."

He shared out the porridge, giving her an extra portion. It poured out of the pot without trepidation. It was perfection.

They sat on the back stoop to savor the victory and watch the sun take its place as the day broke. The porridge was so good. The mix of banana, cinnamon, nutmeg, and milk was everything she needed. She didn't realize how fast she was eating until he grabbed her hand with the spoon.

"Tek time. Mind yuh choke," he said, chuckling.

She chuckled too. He was right, she thought. Goddie then realized that in life, all things can begin anew.

She didn't need the porridge to feel warm inside. Daadie made her feel that way already.

# PART III

# NINE NIGHT

# CHAPTER 10

# COLONGOLOOK RIVER

———

Lincoln drew back the curtains to the room and yelled, "Goddie. GODDIE!" she didn't even flinch. He ran and shook his sister. "Yuh not getting up? Yuh not going to school? A bwoy name James is waiting for you at the gate. Since when yuh go ah school suh early?"

Goddie shot straight up. "Whuh time is?" The window shutters were closed, so she missed her morning wake-up call.

The morning breeze blew a little heavier this morning. The sun delayed its appearance, but the trees resumed their duties. The winds had something to share, but it would have to wait.

Goddie had been up all night. What eluded her all quarter had now come back for a rematch. Today was geometry test day. They both worked hard to overcome the challenging areas, and today was the day to reap. No more late-night sessions. No more studying by bottle torch. Today would prove either fantastic or fatal.

"Six-thirty, dundahead. Nuh make the bwoy wait 'pon you. He is at the gate. I'll go and inspect him," Lincoln said as he walked out of the room.

"Eh bwoy, don't you dare," Goddie yelled as she threw on her uniform and fixed the hornet's nest on her head. She wiped the drool off the corner of her mouth and scrubbed her face with the wet rag on the nail.

Oversleeping for the most important midterm of the year wasn't in the plan, but that's where she found herself. She double-checked her face and hair since a part of her wanted to be presentable for the walk with James. She gathered her books together, slung the bag over her shoulder, and bounded out of her room, stepping over her brothers in the process.

There was Daadie and Mumma standing at the bottom of the steps.

Mumma handed her a tied-up cloth with some warm dumplings and a tin of saltfish. Daadie stood behind Mumma, smirking. Goddie couldn't tell if they were smiling about the test or her escort to school. Either way, she did not have time to figure it out.

"Don't forget to pray before the test, beloved." Mumma said.

"Tell James hello," Daadie chimed.

Mumma looked over at Daadie. "Yuh having too much fun. Leave her alone. Yuh don't have goats tuh move?'"

Daadie kept up the chuckling as he wandered around the side of the house.

Goddie ran down the path to meet up with James. As she approached, his back was turned to her. The sound of her shoes slapping the ground announced her presence.

"Morning. Yuh ready to mashup the test?" asked James.

Goddie looked back to see if Lincoln had followed. "I'm as ready as I'm ever going to be. Let's go before my big-head brother starts an inquiry."

They walked along quietly until James broke the silence.

"The most important thing is that yuh try yuh best and read the questions carefully," he warned.

As the two walked down the path, Goddie began to recite all the different geometry rules to herself, practicing over and over again. Repetition always deepened the impression.

"I want to go a different way to school. We can see the river that way. Is it ok?" James asked.

"Sure. As long as yuh don't make me late for school," Goddie replied. Goddie switched the weight of the books to her other shoulder and picked up her stride.

The two took off behind Goddie's neighbor's house. Getting to the river meant cutting through the district backyards, so they proceeded with caution.

James led the way behind Grandma Anna's house and through the district rep's front yard. They slid past uncle Monroe's gate and ran through the garden to the clearing. Once they cleared the district and the yard dogs, the river awaited them.

They needed to cross at the trellis bridge in order to get to school. As she walked along the bank, Goddie watched the river flow. She knew of the Colongolook River, but now she was seeing its fury up close. The roaring water gave warning to all who would dare, and the current and slippery shoreline made Goddie's trek dangerous. She could hear her heart pounding in her ears from the nerves.

Once they cleared the bend, the trellis bridge appeared. It swayed back and forth, threatening collapse with each step. Goddie swallowed her regret and proceeded on the venture.

"I'll go first. You follow," James instructed. He grabbed the wood rails and calculated every step as the bridge teased him for fun. Goddie followed. If anything happened to James, they would blame her forever. She watched his every step above watching her own.

"Please, God, mek it hold," she whispered. She stopped midway and looked under her feet. The wooden slats hid nothing. She saw the furor, and the furor saw her. She would not be warned again. The swaying bridge broke her gaze, and she exhaled as she finished the cross.

James complained, "Now I've got to pee. Meh can't hold it. Wait here." He didn't wait for an answer before he ran into the bushes.

With the sun barely showing up for duty, Goddie found a dry spot and sat down. Waiting for James gave her time to look. The water sure was moving fast. It had rained the night before, so the current was strong. But it was also interesting to see how the current acknowledged the environment.

Goddie felt hypnotized as she studied how the currents washed over the rocks and gathered the sediment. She took note of the plants that grew up through the sediment bed and up out of the water. Although they were buffeted by the currents, the water had to navigate around the plants and not vice versa. The more the water beat the plants, the higher the resistance.

She could hear Daadie's voice in her head. It was a reminder of what he had said many weeks ago. The Colongolook was a metaphor for life. Much like life, the river's force sought to remove that which wasn't rooted. The river took that which wasn't sure and removed that which wasn't needed. It washed it out into the ocean and strengthened what remained. Goddie sat and thought. Life removes things so that what remains could be clearly seen.

"Yuh want go to school, or yuh want to gaze at the water?" James snapped. "I think we've had enough adventure for one morning."

Goddie brushed off the front of her uniform and followed James down the path to the school. She stayed close to him, but the sound of the river stayed close to her. As they made their way down the cart path and through the churchyard, James encouraged her to relax.

"Yuh upset wid me, James?" asked Goddie.

"No. I just want to get to school so yuh can get ready for the test," he replied. Eventually, the pair crossed the threshold of the school doors.

"Well, well…what do we 'ave here? I see two early birds a try tuh catch di worm. How are yuh dis mawning, Miss. Ormsby? Ready?" Mrs. Gabriel inquired.

Goddie straightened her spine, brushed her uniform front, and looked her teacher straight in the eye. "Bring the test, ma'am. I'm ready."

Their successful morning river crossing gave Goddie a new wave of bravery. She wasn't scared of the misery that was Mrs. Gabriel or the test that awaited them.

The two scholars sat in the desolate classroom exploiting the extra study time before the rest of their classmates showed up. As the rest of the class assembled, Mrs. Gabriel called the class to order. After the morning announcements, it was time.

As Goddie scanned the test before her, she knew she was prepared. She attacked the exam and completed it within the allotted time, but not before James completed his.

He looked back at Goddie and smiled. She smiled and nodded in agreement. He gave her a wink and looked ahead. The wink made her forget she was in class for a second, but she shook it off.

Mrs. Gabriel tapped her desk with a rock. "Ok…test done. Pass the papers up tuh di front, please."

As Mrs. Gabriel started collecting the papers, Goddie heard the murmur of nervous chatter coming from her classmates. She crossed her arms in quiet confidence and waited. Mrs. Gabriel collected her paper, gave her a slight smile, and proceeded with the day's lessons.

Goddie's mind wandered throughout the rest of the day's lessons. She was only concerned about the results of the geometry test. The hours crawled by. As the final bell rang, she rushed up to the teacher's desk to see if Mrs. Gabriel could mark her exam right away.

Despite normal protocol, she complied and pulled out Goddie's test and began to grade it.

"You two can wait at the door of the classroom so I can concentrate. Yuh two love to bother mi eh?" quipped Mrs. Gabriel.

"Yes, ma'am," came the unison voices as they walked outside the classroom.

"Yuh want some?" Goddie said as she broke out the dumplings and saltfish Mumma had given her that morning. She didn't even get the words out good before James was all the way in the fish.

"I shouldn't give yuh any of dis for making me cross that rhaatid bridge this morning," Goddie said.

James laughed and took another dumpling.

Goddie watched as he got busy with the dumpling. James was a good friend. Sometimes in the islands, people develop a crab mentality. Like crabs, when one finds success, the other is ready to pull them back down. That wasn't the case with him.

Goddie swung her head around the corner to see how far along the teacher was in marking the test.

"If you poke yuh head in here again, I mek yuh mop this whole class," advised Mrs. Gabriel.

Goddie took her up on the offer anyway. James was again recruited into helping, not to mention walking her home. Goddie worked slowly to give Mrs. Gabriel time to review her questions.

"Ok, you two, I'm done," Mrs. Gabriel said as she raised her hand to get their attention.

Goddie walked toward her, searching her teacher's face for any early indications. Mrs. Gabriel handed Goddie the sheet of paper. James stayed off in the distance, pretending to clean.

James eventually shimmied his way along the wall to get a better view. There was a pregnant pause in the classroom, and then Goddie turned her head and held the passing grade up. Her smile lit up the room.

"B plus James," Goddie gushed.

James's teeth lit up the room too.

Mrs. Gabriel nodded her head in agreement and continued grading the other papers. Then she said, "Now the two of you get out." As Goddie ran out the door, Mrs. Gabriel called her back into the class. "Congratulations, Miss Ormsby. Well earned. Keep the grip on yuh studies."

"Yes, ma'am. Yes, ma'am."

Goddie took another moment to look at the test paper and soak in the glory. She had worked hard for her grade. She gave James a big hug and put the paper in her school bag. But her joy was suddenly interrupted.

Goddie's classmate Delroy burst into the classroom, grabbing Goddie's arm. "Why yuh still here, Goddie! Everyone a look fi yuh. Come now."

Annoyed, she pulled her arm back, "Why?"

"There's be an accident. He's gone."

"Who's gone?"

"Cousin Chris dead from this mawnin. Colongolook took him," replied Delroy.

"Daadie?" whispered Goddie.

"Yes. It's yuh Daadie. Let's go."

## CHAPTER 11

# COUSIN CHRIS

———

The pounding of the concrete underneath her feet was the only indicator she was still moving. Goddie looked back for James, but he had fallen behind. Everything around her seemed to slow down as she ran through the schoolyard and turned to make the journey home.

"If dis is a joke, I'm gonna beat yuh. 'ear me?" she yelled as she struggled to keep up with Delroy.

His firm grip on her wrist told Goddie he was serious. Her school bag swung from one side to the other without discretion. Their desire to cut through backyards was curtailed by mean dogs and high fences. Instead, they would have to take the long way and go around.

Delroy dragged Goddie up the main support road to Shatimy Crossing and around the bend. As she tried to find a balance between being dragged and running out of breath, the film of her life ran through her mind.

All the moments with her father seemed insurmountable. *How could this be? Daadie is gone?*

As she made her way home, the surroundings began to change. While she had no physical confirmation of his death, Spring Hill told her something was wrong.

As they ran through the district, all she could hear was Delroy yelling to keep up and her pounding heart.

Goddie glanced around and noticed the children weren't playing. They were just standing and staring.

Even the trees standing guard over the district bowed in reverence to what she was about to affirm. The merchants didn't trade. The mothers didn't gossip. Even the postman stopped sorting as she ran by.

The district was quiet.

The pair wound their way through Spring Hill and ran alongside the river. The Colongolook River flowed quietly without event. Her face asked the question, but the river offered no indictments or exonerations.

"Something must have really happened," she whispered between gulps of air. Delroy had not broken stride once.

"Come on, Goddie. Keep up, mon. Stop gazin'," he responded as his grip tightened and his stride lengthened.

She only saw the back of his head, but she could hear him clearly. As they continued the journey home, Goddie noticed even the road itself paid honor to her father.

She didn't remember leaving the river and running up the hill, but somehow, she found herself at the top.

Delroy finally let go of her hand as they turned down the path toward home. He placed his hands on his knees as he caught his breath. James finally caught up and leaned on a tree for relief. Both watched as Goddie walked ahead toward the Ormsby house.

With each step, Goddie felt her life was about to change. When she got to the gate, her eyes opened wide.

Goddie glanced around, making note of the people standing outside her house. Some were strangers who came to offer help and assistance. The others just came to look and see what the news of the day was. As she scanned left and right, she processed all the faces and all the eyes. She gathered all the expressions and registered them in her memory.

"Who are all these people, Delroy?" Goddie asked.

"Some of them are the people who found your father," he replied as he caught up to her.

"Found my father? Whuh yuh mean?" she asked as she studied the crowd.

"They will tell yuh inside."

She scanned left and right, processing all the faces and all the eyes. She recognized the church mothers off to the side. One held a white sheet over her arm as she dabbed her face. They were dressed in white with a white head wrap. The elders stood beside them, attentive to the moment.

She realized there would be no idle chat today. As she neared the veranda, she dropped her book bag and the crowd in front parted ways in acknowledgment. The gravel softened her steps. She walked slowly up the path and gingerly up the steps to the door frame.

The very air changed when she reached the threshold. She somehow knew if she went forward, her life would be changed forever. For on one side of the doorframe was life, and on the other side of the doorframe was a horror unimaginable.

Goddie focused on his foot. It was all she could see without going any further inside. They had the same foot shape. She inhaled deeply, exhaled slowly, and took a few more steps inside the house.

Lauretta was the first to acknowledge her. "Come, Goddie," she said, as she reached out her hand. "We've been waiting for you. Come say goodbye to Daadie." Confusion washed over Goddie's face as she processed her sister's strange hospitality. She was never this nice to Goddie. It was like watching a peculiar movie.

Goddie stared at her siblings, and they stared back at her. She had never really experienced firsthand the death of anyone. The heaviness of the moment pressed against her chest. Her breathing slowed.

She often heard about this neighbor passing away or that church elder passing away. But it all seemed like such a distant notion to her. It was always someone else somewhere else.

This time it wasn't.

The death angel had stopped at her doorstep this time. She walked further into the house. The sights and sounds became ominous. Nobody was talking. The floor registered her every step.

She walked a few more steps into the room and at last got a full glimpse of her nightmare. There he lay, the general to their army, the bishop to their church, and the father to their family.

They laid him straight on a board in the middle of the room. She stood there and studied him as her eyes slowly scanned from his feet up to his legs. His legs had sand and dirt residue all over, and his muscles didn't command attention as she remembered.

She took note of how his hands were all wrinkly, like dried prunes. *How did he get so wrinkly?* she wondered.

Registering these strange thoughts kept the grief tsunami at bay for a moment. Her eyes continued to scan the rest of his body. His work shorts looked damp, and the floor around him was soaked as well. She forced her eyes to examine the rest of him. She watched his chest. She watched and waited. She watched and waited some more. No movement.

Her eyes finally met his face, and the revelation was complete. He wasn't moving.

Goddie knelt on the floor beside her father, examining him up close. She looked at the side of his face. She watched his temples. Nothing. Grabbing his arm, she leaned in and spoke into his ear.

"Daadie?'"

"Daadie?"

She touched his face with the back of her hand, felt his forehead, and stroked his head. She looked up at all the strangers called brothers and sisters. Her attention then turned back to her hero. She leaned in again.

"Daadie? It's me, Goddie. Daadie?" she pleaded as the tears crept down her face.

She continued to call his name while she stroked his hair and cleaned the dirt from his face. She noticed her baby sister Lassie standing behind Dearis and Minnette.

Lassie's big eyes looked to Goddie for an answer, but Goddie had nothing to give her. As she turned back to her father, she saw the mucus slime mixed with sand on the side of his face. Whatever was in him was now on his face, and nobody even noticed. She could see his gums through his open mouth, and her face became enraged.

"WHAT HAPPENED TO 'IM?" she screamed. Lassie ducked behind her sisters as her older brothers looked down with tears.

"You could at least wipe his face. What de rass good are you? Pass me the rhaatid washcloth," she cursed.

No one dared to scold her for using curse words.

Lambert passed her a wet rag from the table. She grabbed it and wiped Daadie's entire face. She wiped all around his lips and his nose. She wiped his cheeks and forehead before administering her final act of kindness. She closed his mouth.

It was the least she could do after all he had done. She sat back on her legs and looked at him again. She scanned his body up and down—his legs, his arms, and his chest. She had to be sure, so she rested her head on the side of his chest. She listened, hoping to hear something. A crackle, a bump, a beat. Nothing.

"He's so cold." The tears dropped, and her voice skipped its cadence. She shook her head in refusal.

"He's so cold. He's so cold," she looked up at Lambert. He stood there, silent.

As she came to herself, the gravity of the reality set in and she released herself. She wept without cognizance. Her young body heaved as she struggled for air to feed her sobbing. She opened her mouth and called for her father in earnest. The room erupted as Goddie was the final lynchpin to the flood gates.

Daadie was gone. He was gone.

Lauretta left the wall she was holding up to bring Goddie some water. Goddie looked into her eldest sister's eyes. "What happened to him, Lauretta? He was fine this morning."

"Dem find him by the riverside this morning. Dem seh he fell in the river and went under. Some people were able to pull him out, but he took on some water and couldn't get it out. The current was too strong."

Goddie's eyes lit up. "So why Delroy just come for me? Yuh knew about dis all day? ALL DAY?"

Lauretta walked back to the wall she was determined to hold up. No one came off the wall to clear Goddie's confusion. They were all complicit.

"I was the one who told dem not to tell yuh. I knew today was important for yuh schooling. Blame me," said Lauretta.

Goddie's stare tore through her sister. Lambert stood beside Lauretta, nodding in support, but it didn't matter to Goddie.

The wailing in the next room was unmistakable. Goddie could not bring herself to process anymore. Her father was dead, and that was all she could handle. The elders outside discussed what happened among themselves, but that was of no consequence to her now.

The strangest part about looking at Daadie lying on the plank was the simple fact that he was still. She remembered how he was always moving. He was always working. He was always cooking something, lifting something, moving something, or cleaning something.

He was the survival of Jamaica personified. A warrior that had gone to battle with life itself and now was called to rest. He was so still, but in a strange way, she was glad because at least he was finally getting his rest. It was a strange thought for her, but it was an honest one.

"What are we to do now?" Goddie asked.

No one responded.

"Lincoln, what are we to do now?" He didn't have an answer.

She looked at her brothers, and they looked at each other. They grew more pathetic to her with every moment.

The wailing in the next room pierced the silence. The faces that met her on the way in were now looking through the windows. So many eyes having so few answers. Fear began to grip her body. She felt herself tightening up. As she realized the weight of the moment, the tears flowed heavier.

She continued to stroke his head and wipe his face. She leaned over and whispered in his ear. "Thank yuh, Daadie. Thank yuh. Mi will love yuh forever." She kissed his forehead and wiped his face one last time.

At that moment, she felt alone. She looked at her father again and kissed him on his forehead. She sighed and rubbed his face. As she rose and made the three or four steps to the corner of the room, her head became heavy as her legs gave out from under her. Lincoln and Vurley caught her just in time.

The district mothers came in and covered the body, and the elders quietly grabbed the four corners of the plank. After a moment of silence, they rose to carry him away.

The siblings held each other and watched as their general, their bishop, and their father, left for the last time.

The grief churned from every organ, through every molecule, and manifested itself through her vocal cords to her lips and beyond her teeth. It was a sound unspeakable. A rage undeniable. A fear untenable. Daadie was gone.

For Goddie, feeling all alone was a strange notion when she had eight siblings and a mother. He was the only one who understood who she was. He was her biggest advocate and sometimes her best friend.

*So what will become of us?* She wondered. As the last remnants of him crossed the threshold into the night, she turned her attention toward the wailing in the other room.

Mumma was inconsolable. She was unrecognizable. The sounds she uttered were from another world. The tears she cried were guttural. Goddie could do nothing for her. She leaned against the wall of the room and looked at her mother, knowing Mumma's life had changed forever. They had been together for over twenty-five years. Daadie never left her side. Now he was gone.

After a while, the crowd dissipated into the night and the well-wishers took their leave. The heat of August gave no reprieve to death, and the breeze was anaemic.

As Mumma finally fell asleep, the house became quiet. The stress of the evening had exhausted everyone. There were no tears left. Everyone was exhausted. Silence was the balm now.

Goddie walked through the house to the veranda for some air. She turned to the left and saw the school bag Delroy had brought in. She picked it up and sat on the front stoop, staring out into the night sky and watching the peeny wallies light up the front field.

James wandered up the path and sat beside her. As the two stared off into the field, she rubbed her hands together, slapped her thigh, and began to weep. In her bag was the passing math grade she wanted to share with Daadie.

Goddie put her face in her hands.

Daadie was gone.

## CHAPTER 12

# NINE NIGHT

——

The days after Daadie's death were the most frustrating and upsetting for Goddie. The district carried on with business as usual. The events just eight days ago didn't weigh as heavy on the district now as they did then.

Eventually, smiles returned to the district citizens and activity rebounded. The shock had worn off, and the grieving was left up to the Ormsby family. Everyone reverted to minding their own business. Small chat was limited, and speculative gossip was prohibited.

Goddie wandered aimlessly through the days. Some days she had forgotten to bathe, even though Minnette kept reminding her.

The Colongolook River offered no apology as it welcomed back the swimmers and mothers doing laundry. Many in the district hurried about their duties as the nine-night wake for Daadie was to occur that evening.

The nine-night celebration was a Jamaican tradition. It was said that it took nine days for the spirit of the departed to leave the body. The party on the ninth night was to finally send off the spirit for good. Its origins in African culture were not in question as much as what was on the menu for the night.

The culmination of cooked meats, ground provisions, and rum could soothe any grieving soul. It was the final time for the community to come together in love to celebrate Daadie's life, say farewell to his spirit, and support the clan.

For Goddie, it was just a reason to have more work to do than normal. She begrudgingly went through the motions but was resigned that all these rituals wouldn't bring her father back.

She stared off into the field as she swayed her hand in the pot full of rice and water. As she rinsed rice for the feast, her mind entertained daydreams of Daadie moving goats from one side of the field to the other.

Her hand movements synchronized with her memories as she recalled his counsel and his chastisement. The cloudy rice water caught her tears as her thoughts re-emerged from the murk of uncertainty to the reality of what was. As the rice grains flowed through her fingers, so did every moment she had with her Daadie.

With each swirl, she conjured up another memory, another recollection of simpler days. As she repositioned the pot between her legs and continued swirling her dreams under closed eyes, her ears snapped her back to reality.

Lauretta swung open the veranda door and asked, "How long are yuh going to ramp wid dat rice?"

"Huh?"

"Di rice is clean now," Lauretta barked as she snatched the pot from Goddie. "Here, peel dis. Nuh baddah cut off yuh finger and hurry up. Di people dem soon come."

Goddie snapped out of her grief to see the washed rice replaced with washed yams and a knife. She looked up to see Dearis and Lassie wandering over. The younger girls hadn't spent much time with her since Daadie passed, and it was just as well.

She barely had the patience for herself, let alone those two. But they were her sisters, and she knew they needed her even though she didn't feel like needing them.

Dearis started first. "Mumma keeps crying."

Goddie sighed and said, "I know."

Lassie chimed second. "Mumma keeps calling fi Daadie."

Goddie closed her eyes and said, "I know."

As she peeled away, Goddie sat back and listened to their concerns and questions. She tried to answer them as best as she could.

Dearis pondered aloud, "If Daadie is gone and Mumma keeps crying, who is taking care of us?"

"I am," replied Goddie.

Lassie piped in, "Good, cuz Lauretta's mout too loud and she gwaan like she ah big person." She crossed her arms and looked over at Dearis.

Dearis looked over at Lassie and pulled her in closer.

"Don't worry yuh self Lassie. Goddie will tek care of me, and I'll take special care of yuh. We'll be just fine," encouraged Dearis.

Goddie pondered what would become of her and her siblings.

Every once in a while, Lauretta would walk into the room and bring Mumma some soup and walk back out. Mumma was despondent. She was incoherent to the realities of life on a farm in Jamaica, advocating her duties to the eldest children and her care to the goodness of strangers.

Lambert and Lincoln took the lead to ensure there was food and money for school fees. Even Reynold tagged along with his brothers to help move the goats and tend the fields. The harvesting of the crop in the afternoon took up most of their time. The distraction allowed them to step away from their grief, even if for a few moments, and take care of the younger ones.

As Goddie continued peeling yams, she saw Lambert working the land in the distance. His body frame was undeniable, and his stride was a sure giveaway. He walked just like Daadie.

He walked toward her carrying some cut-up sugar cane stalks for the nine-night gathering. As he closed the gap, Goddie could see the events of the past eight days were etched into his face. When he saw his sister, his etched face made way for a smile.

"Has the bashment started early?" Lambert asked, using a new term he picked up from his friends describing a loud party.

"We are the bashment," chimed Dearis and Lassie. The girls giggled to themselves as they sought to make Goddie laugh.

Goddie gave a half smirk in response to their moment of levity. It was ok to have a little fun. Daadie would have wanted that.

Goddie put her serious face back on. "Guh and get washed up before di people dem start come. Dearis, yuh wash up Lassie. Gwaan."

The two sisters hopped up and made their way into the house. As the door opened, the sounds of a slow moan escaped into the late afternoon breeze. Lambert placed the sugar cane to one side and sat down beside Goddie.

"I miss Daadie bad, Lambert," Goddie lamented. She took the knife and started digging into the step. The more upset she got, the deeper she gouged the wood. Lambert finally grabbed her hand and rested it in her lap.

"As do I," he said.

Goddie sighed. "I feel so unsure now. Daadie always did give good wisdom when tings went wrong, and now 'im gone. What are we supposed to do now? Mumma can't stop cry. Field work not done. Tings not going so good, and it's only been a few days."

She knew she would have to navigate alone once Daadie was buried. Her younger siblings offered no support, and her older siblings were trying to figure it out themselves.

Being the middle child offered its challenges. She was the hinge of the family. She was too old to tolerate baby siblings and too young to ever be pledged into the older siblings' club.

If there was a silver lining in the death of Daadie, it was that it accelerated Goddie's desire to seek and do something different. She didn't want to be in Jamaica, waiting on the next person to die. If she was going to live, she was going to live on her own terms.

She had already received permission from Daadie, and she didn't need permission from anyone else. With her thoughts racing, Goddie sighed and leaned against the porch pillar.

Lambert came closer and put his arm around his sister. His comfort felt so familiar. The tears flowed quietly for both siblings as they looked out into the field. Goddie leaned into her brother and resumed peeling yams.

"I better get this cane inside. Lauretta is waiting for it," Lambert said. He looked over at his sister, and she slowly looked over at him. His half smile broke the sadness, and he gave her a squeeze before shifting his weight to stand up.

"Goddie, your life isn't over. Wuh yuh life has for yuh is still out deh. Yuh may be di little one, but yuh are also di stronger one. You look up to us, but we are watching yuh as well. We all must learn to start again. It's sad now, but we will be ok," explained Lambert.

Goddie looked up at Lambert. "Start again?"

"Yes. Start again," Lambert responded, looking her straight in the eye. "That's what Daadie would have wanted all of us to do. Rise and start again." With that, he collected his cargo and stepped past her inside the house.

It wouldn't be long before Lauretta came looking for the yams, so she grabbed the last one in the bowl and started in on it. It was the largest yam of the bunch, so she had trouble holding and peeling it. She repositioned the piece so many times it eventually slipped out her hand and rolled down the path a few feet.

"Even the yam dem want to leave Daadie. Even the yam knows," she whispered. Goddie went after the runaway vegetable. She quickly finished peeling and headed inside.

First, she had to peek in on Mumma, although she didn't know what to say. She hadn't spoken to her mother in a few days. She peered between the cracks into the room. She saw Mumma in bed looking at the wall. Mumma seemed so confused.

Goddie realized the best of Mumma had died with Daadie. All of Mumma's humor, energy, and poise went away when Daadie died. She could no longer coherently give instructions or lead the family. She hadn't cooked for days, and based on the trays of food, she hadn't eaten for days either.

Whether she would be able to reengage with the family was yet to be decided. At the end of the day, she was still Mumma, and Goddie needed to ensure that she would be okay. It was decided later that Lauretta and Minnette would tend to Mumma's daily needs, and Goddie would keep the young ones in line.

Goddie's thoughts were interrupted by the shadow of a strange man knocking on the veranda frame. He looked somewhat familiar, but she wasn't sure. Lauretta pushed past her to greet the gentleman, and Lambert soon followed.

Goddie slowly walked through the house to the veranda and watched as her brother and sister talked to the gentleman. Lauretta's hand motions and Lambert's loud voice told Goddie they were talking about burying Daadie. She watched as the gentleman walked away and her brother and sister walked back toward the house.

"We are not going to have enough to do all that, Lauretta. We can do a simple burial, but a headstone is an entirely different ting altogether," complained Lambert as he walked past Goddie back into the house.

"We'll just do what we gotta do," consoled Lauretta. "Mek wah we have work. That's it." Lauretta pushed past Goddie and into the room to update Mumma.

"No headstone?" asked Mumma. Goddie slipped alongside the door frame to catch the conversation.

"No headstone," replied Lauretta as Lambert walked past his nosey sister into Mumma's bedroom.

"We'll bury him by the black mango tree to mark the site, Mumma. That's all we can do. We don't have the money," explained Lauretta.

Lambert walked out of the bedroom and leaned against the wall.

"Blacks can't afford to live in this life, and they can't afford to leave it either," he said.

"What's wrong?" questioned Goddie.

"Life is expensive. Death is expensive. The cost of building Daadie's tomb and preparing the body for burial is too much. We can't afford to do everything," Lambert complained.

He wiped his tears and pushed off from the wall. All this talk about Daadie, burials, work assignments, and Mumma had reached its height. Nine night was tonight, and the burial was tomorrow. Whatever was going to happen, Daadie would still be dead, and the rest would just be a conversation.

Goddie headed to the outdoor kitchen as the district residents began to gather for the nine-night festivities. Everyone was positioned for a good time, but Goddie wasn't positioned for anything.

The bottles of rum were stacked up, and the smell of escovitch fish saturated the night. Lincoln and Vurley stacked up more wood for the kitchen, and Minnette kept an eye on Lassie.

They were sending Daadie off Jamaican style, but Goddie couldn't care less. Strangers were no replacement for her father.

Lauretta stacked the jerk chicken, and Lambert kept pace with the soup. Goddie reached between them to grab a chicken leg and started walking down the path. As she walked, she saw James walking toward her with food. He stopped right in front of her, but she just walked past him.

"Yuh not staying for the nine night, Goddie? Everybody is coming, mon," James said.

"No," Goddie mumbled as she walked straight by him.

"Dis a fi yuh father. Yuh nuh want tuh stay?"

"Yuh can have di bashment. Daadie is already right here with me," Goddie replied as she disappeared into the night. James watched her as long as he could before he turned and went up to the house.

As the sun finally set, the evening breeze took its time blowing through Spring Hill. It was in no hurry. It had been a long week for the Ormsby clan, and tonight they would say farewell to Daadie's spirit.

Tomorrow they would say farewell to his body.

# CHAPTER 13

# BLACK MANGO TREE

——

The mix of rain and heat throughout the parish that morning made for an unwelcome guest in an already unwelcome situation.

Uncle Monroe borrowed a truck that would bring Daadie to the Birnamwood churchyard for the service. Goddie could always count on her uncle to help. He always stood in the gap when Daadie wasn't around.

When it was time to head to the churchyard, there wasn't enough room on the truck. Goddie and her siblings decided to make the slow walk down the hill.

The villagers from all over the district came to honor cousin Chris. They all lined up along the side of the road as the siblings advanced toward to the churchyard. The merchants stopped trading, and the mothers stopped gossiping just long enough to bow their heads in reverence.

Daadie was a kind soul. He was always active in the community and ready to help and be useful. Goddie knew his altruism personified the best of Spring Hill. Even in death, he brought strangers together.

Lassie pulled on Goddie's dress. "I can't see. The rain is falling in my eyes."

Goddie looked down. The six-year-old was soaked from head to toe.

Her one good pair of church shoes sloshed with every step. As they continued the walk, Lassie grabbed her hand. This would be her first funeral. Goddie squeezed her hand tight and gave her the same half smile Lambert had given Goddie one day earlier.

"Yuh stand wid mi. Ok?" said Goddie.

Lassie nodded her head and picked up her pace.

The rain fell without concession, saturating grievers and onlookers alike. The closer they got to the church, the heavier the rain fell.

As they walked together down the path, the district assembled close to say farewell to Daadie. Some residents joined the Ormsbys as the siblings walked in silence to bury their general.

The coconut trees of the district gave as much canopy as possible. They bowed once again in condolence as Goddie looked up in appreciation. Every step she took was sacred. She would never march these steps again for another father.

The truck carrying Daadie drove slowly alongside the Colongolook River. From the road, Goddie could see people bathing in the same spot they had found Daadie. It was a strange feeling to be angry at a river for being a river.

"Yuh tek Daadie," Goddie muttered. "Nuh badda tek nobady else." With that, she turned her head, and the river turned away as well. They both had an understanding.

By the time Goddie could see the turn into the churchyard, all of Spring Hill was waiting there to greet them. The earth had been dug up and moved to the side. The drizzle off the black mango tree became a deluge. A mud stream ran from the tree and met Goddie at the church gate.

Others followed behind her, and the singing soon became wailing. As she looked around and studied the faces, Goddie understood that this moment was beyond her. She looked over her shoulder, and her knees weakened. There they were, the majority of Spring Hill soaked to the skin, standing in agreement with her and her siblings.

"Mi never know Daadie knew so many people," Lassie whispered to Goddie.

"Mi never know either," replied Goddie.

The crying died down long enough to catch the last stanza of the hymn:

*"When Christ shall come, with a shout of acclamation,*
*And take me home, what joy shall fill my heart.*
*Then I shall bow, in humble adoration,*
*And then proclaim: "My God, how great Thou art!*

*Then sings my soul, My Saviour God, to Thee,*
*How great Thou art, How great Thou art.*
*Then sings my soul, My Saviour God, to Thee,*
*How great Thou art, How great Thou art!"*

Lincoln and Vurley looked back as the chorus of villagers crescendoed. Their eyes were weary from the tears. Goddie's heart swelled with gladness, knowing that he was received.

The elders of the church removed the coffin from the back of the truck. Goddie stared at the simple wooden box. There it was, finality manifested. The nails, the wood fiber, and the very hinges registered her attention. They slowly carried him up the slight hill to his final resting spot under the black mango tree.

The black mango tree in the churchyard was the perfect spot. It was located away from the cluster of other burial plots in the corner of the churchyard.

Goddie had been coming to that churchyard her whole life and never noticed the massive black mango tree off in the corner. Her eyes followed the tree from trunk to crown and branch to branch. She inspected its worthiness as the resting spot for Daadie and determined it worked just fine.

She decided others may have had a headstone, but Daadie had shade during the summer. The tree served its purpose on this day, too, as they needed the shelter from the rain to lay Daadie to rest.

Goddie smiled to herself. Daadie deserved to rest in a good place.

As the family walked behind the casket, Goddie noticed some of the other resting spots of family members. She had never really taken note of the number of Ormsby names on the tombstones.

Goddie noted how well the community had prepared for Daadie's funeral. The schoolhouse that sat beside the church had been cleaned. The church grounds had been cleared. The brethren did a good job preparing the area.

She began to have mixed feelings about this moment. She knew it was coming but didn't know how to interpret it. It was all so much confusion. How could someone she just had breakfast with one day be dead and buried a few days later? It all seemed like nonsense to her.

When they got to the graveside, the hymns got louder. The wailing got louder too.

Goddie watched everything—the crowd movements and the facial expressions. The ceremony became a lesson in cadence for her. She looked around and finally placed her eyes upon Mumma.

There she was, a crumpled heap leaning on Lambert. She looked so thin. She looked weak. She looked older.

Goddie hadn't had a meaningful conversation with Mumma in over a week. She couldn't do anything to be helpful to Mumma, and Mumma certainly couldn't be helpful to her. Goddie realized she was on her own.

After they lowered the casket into the hole, Mumma was the first to throw some dirt. It was customary for the spouse to start the burial process. As the song raised and the tempo increased, Mumma became inconsolable.

When the burial commenced, so did the rain.

As the mourners dispersed, Goddie elected to stay. He had been there with her for her entire life. He never left her, and she wasn't about to leave him. She was staying until the last shovel load was thrown.

As Lauretta carried Mumma away, Goddie watched as the elders and her brothers buried Daadie. With each full shovel, Goddie's siblings began to break down in tears. They knew there was a finite ending to the burial procession.

The deaconess arranged the last of the flowers on top of the dirt mound.

Daadie was laid to rest.

When Goddie walked back down the hill, she received the last of the condolences from strangers and heartfelt messages of the familiar. As the rain intensified, everyone decided to head back to the house. The same truck that brought Daadie to his final resting place was now waiting to bring the family back to the farm.

Goddie watched as everyone piled into the back of the truck. Lincoln waved for Goddie to hurry up and catch the ride. She waved them on. She didn't want any company. She felt bad for leaving Daadie all alone.

She outstretched her arm and waved. "Bye, Daadie. Bye, Daad…. Bye, Daa," she sobbed.

She turned around and walked toward the exit gate. As she walked through the churchyard, she passed both the school and the church where she spent most of her life.

Approaching the gate, she grabbed the post and looked back one more time at the gravesite. The rain was no match for her tears. She sighed and began the long walk up the hill.

The truck was still waiting, but she waved them to go on. The driver waved back, and the truck disappeared into the downpour. She was adamant about walking the hill by herself.

She would have to get used to walking up hills alone.

"Bye, Daadie," she whispered. With that, Goddie disappeared into the storm.

## CHAPTER 14

# FRACTURED

———

Goddie rested herself on the windowsill. She took pleasure in the afternoon rain hitting her forearms. It had been a while since she just looked at herself. Her long arms took up the windowsill, and the coconut oil she put on that morning caused the drops to bead as the rain played drums on her arm.

Blue Mountain suffered an aggressive rainy season, and the storms saturated the Ormsby farm. Goddie watched the deluge come every day like an advancing Greek army. No retreat. No surrender.

Her brothers tried to rescue the remaining crops, but it was impossible work. Harvesting crops in saturated soil meant the work took twice as long, with fewer crops to show for the effort. Nevertheless, it had to be done. Yams, coffee beans, and sugar cane couldn't harvest themselves.

Goddie wiped the hair on her forearm and smiled. Daadie had the same forearm hair. She never really noticed until now. She listened to the thunder hammering the afternoon sky and tossed dried coffee beans as far as they could go.

There was mercy in the mundane. For a few weeks, she could just be a sixteen-year-old girl trying to figure out life. For a few weeks, she let her older siblings be the adults, and she co-oped her baby siblings' care to the neighbors. She needed some time to herself.

The weeks after burying Daadie were quiet. Everyone was tired. The peace didn't last long though, Lambert made sure of that. Even through the rain, Goddie could make out her older brother storming up to Lincoln in front of the house.

"DOCTAH! Yuh miss di pickup again!" Lambert yelled. "Dis a di third time yuh not ready tuh load di truck. How can we sell at di market if we can't git tuh di market? Tell me nuh?" The only time Lambert used Lincoln's pet name was when he was angry. The weight of Lambert's argument was heavy. He sounded scared.

Lincoln shot back. "Evah since Daadie dead, yuh have been on mi like a slave. Tired of it now. Yuh are not mi Daadie. 'im dead already. Gwaan call Vurley to be yuh slave."

The tension between the brothers had been simmering for weeks. Daadie always commanded respect from his sons and got the work of the farm done. The understanding of roles after Daadie died was complicated.

Suddenly, the students were forced to become teachers and the conveyance of values was left to those still figuring out their own lives. When it was Daadie and Mumma, there was a natural progression of things. With Daadie gone and Mumma wrapped in bed, what was once natural now became forced.

"Doctah, if we nuh sell, we nuh eat. What sells at di market pays di land lease and school fees," Lambert explained.

Goddie heard school fees and leaned in closer.

Lambert continued, "I'm not trying to be Daadie. Mi jus a try tuh mek sure wi can feed ourselves. We have to work together. Tek some of these vegetables to the back. We have fi cook dem before dem spoil now. Hurrah up, Doctah." The argument was so intense, it drowned out the sound of the rain.

From the window, Goddie could see all the ground provisions meant for the market piled up. Now they were all getting soaked and soon no good for anyone.

Over the past few weeks, Lincoln had become disenchanted with Spring Hill. He had taken a few trips to Kingston, where his friends showed him where he could make more money. The promise of work in the big city was attractive, but the reality of finding work was far from it. Nevertheless, Lincoln's disengagement with the needs of the farm was beginning to show.

Lincoln started down the path to salvage the vegetables. His bare feet disappeared in the mud with each step. His soaked shirt clung to him like skin. He adjusted his sagging pants before he turned his head back toward Lambert.

"Just so yuh know, mi dream is NOT to be a farmer. I don't want it. Mi soon gone from here. When do I get to be me?"

Lambert dropped his head and walked in the rain around to the side of the house. The weight was too much. Lincoln finally saw Goddie in the window and their eyes locked. She gave him a dirty look.

He wiped his face and turned around in disgust. Goddie watched him until he disappeared. Her eyes left Lincoln and trailed to the ground. Her thoughts drifted as she watched the raindrops compete for space in the dirt.

*Daadie, what is happening to the family? Everybody is fading away from each other. Anger is the new family member, and everyone has made it feel welcome. We are losing our way. We don't know each other. We will not last like this. We just won't.*

Goddie wiped her tears with her dress just in time to notice Lauretta and Minnette carrying a pan of water and a broom out of Mumma's room. She had been avoiding Mumma for days. Between fits of crying, angry bursts, and long slumbers, Mumma was difficult to get close to.

Something was going on inside her body nobody was acknowledging. Sickness was always a secret in Portland. Ever since Daadie died, Mumma wasn't eating. She drank water constantly and was always on the bedpan. She used that bedpan so much, Uncle Monroe had to find another one.

Lauretta was always changing the sheets, and Lambert mentioned something about her kidneys. Mumma lost a lot of weight. All the weight in her arms was gone, and her housedress barely hung on her. Mumma's hips looked smaller, and Goddie could see her shoulder blades clearly.

Comprehending what happened to Mumma was the most turbulent part of Daadie's death. His death was not hard to understand, as horrible as it was. But Mumma's decompensation was beyond Goddie's ability to process. Mumma's light simply disappeared. Like a candle in an open window, Mumma illuminated no more.

Goddie eased herself off the window, brushed the front of her dress, and slowly trekked to her mother's room.

Just a few months ago, she had no problem bounding into that room and chiseling her way onto her parents' bed. It was hard for Daadie to get upset when the puppy eyes were looking up at him.

It was all different now.

Mumma's room was a strange place. A cozy hideaway was now a sparse vacant room with an equally vacant occupant—a solitary sanctuary capturing the constant wail of a woman in pain. The panels of the room walls served dual purposes now. The frail wood frame now served to keep the elements out and the wails of a fractured woman in. The wood flooring was no friend as it announced every step Goddie took toward her mother.

When Goddie parted the curtain, she saw a strange person sitting on Mumma's bed. The person she saw was frail. She looked exhausted. The person Goddie saw had the weight of the world on her shoulders.

Over the last few weeks, Mumma didn't eat anything meaningful. She stared deeply, her eyes scanning from side to side searching for somebody. Every few hours, she walked her room whispering, "Chris."

Goddie figured she was searching for Daadie. Goddie could understand that. She was searching for Daadie too. Mumma remained in a state of loss and bewilderment. The trauma of Daadie's death took her somewhere where reality didn't live.

Her love was gone, and she was alone in a house with nine strangers. Goddie just studied her.

*Daadie, Mumma is looking for you. She's hurting. She's confused. She cries for you constantly and wails at your absence. I don't know what to do. It's scary. She's not Mumma anymore.*

Goddie walked further into the room. She rounded the bed corner far enough to get a good look at her mother. Goddie could see the fear in her eyes. Mumma looked so vulnerable.

Goddie always remembered Mumma as the strong one, the one who never spared a moment to share a kind word or an encouraging thought. So, there she sat, a shell of herself, waiting for the next verdict. She looked scary to Goddie. It was hard for her not to be scared for her mother. Goddie leaned in close.

"Hi, Mumma."

"Is you Lauretta?" Mumma turned her head to the side to listen better.

"No, Mumma, it's me, Goddie."

Mumma turned her face even more from the window, "Who name suh? Mi nuh know nobody named Goddie."

Goddie raised her eyebrows in disbelief. She looked around the room, out the window, and back at Mumma.

*Mumma doesn't know me? She doesn't see me? Mumma tun mad woman?* Goddie thought.

Tears began to well in Goddie's eyes. As the tears fell on her housedress, she edged herself in front of her mother. Goddie stared at her from head to toe. Mumma's thick plaits had given way to a knotty mess. The strong arms that used to knead dumplings were no longer. They were just lean sinews of themselves, barely able to hold her hand to her head.

Goddie watched as Mumma stood up and shuffled around the room. She dragged her feet, shuffling from one place to another while her breath shallowed and her energy waned.

*Daadie, what should I do? Mumma is scaring me. She's scary, Daadie. She doesn't know who I am anymore.*

Goddie studied Mumma. She had her Mumma's fingertips, the creases in her hand, and the length of her forearms. Mumma was long and beautiful. If only she knew she could literally hug herself. She could comfort herself.

"Are yuh going to be ok, Mumma?" she asked.

Her mother shifted her eyes once again to acknowledge the stranger and gave her a slow nod.

Goddie offered her a cup of water. Mumma took the cup with two hands and put it to her mouth. She swallowed and shifted her eyes back toward the window. Goddie watched her throat move in acknowledgment. It was all about the details now.

Goddie adjusted her position on the bed and accepted reality. She focused her eyes on her mother, taking in her every nuance. It all became clear. She would bear witness to two deaths, except this one would be the long goodbye.

A tear rolled down Goddie's cheek. She grabbed a brush off the side table and started brushing her Mumma's hair. She didn't know what else to do. Mumma's hair was starting to dread. Nevertheless, it was either an opportunity to spend time with her or a desperate attempt to be helpful.

As she brushed her hair slowly, Goddie sang a hymn. As the hymn progressed, Mumma closed her eyes and rocked back and forth. She put her hands together and began rubbing her fingers. This was all she needed. Mumma needed someone to take care of her for a moment and allow her soul to stop searching for comfort, even for a moment.

Goddie grabbed the coconut oil tin and started rubbing some on her mother's neck and back. It wasn't much in task, but it was enough in thought. Mumma reached up with her right hand and stopped Goddie's hand with a tap.

"Thank you, Veta."

Goddie stopped cold. She tilted her head to look at the side of her mother's face. Mumma hadn't called Goddie by her birth name in years. Goddie almost didn't recognize it herself.

"Almost done, Mumma. Duh yuh need anyting else?" Goddie asked, wiping the oil off her hands.

"No. Thanks, Veta."

Goddie looked up again. She looked behind her to see Lauretta and Lambert looking on. They heard her too.

"She never calls you Veta," Lambert whispered.

Lauretta turned her head to look at Lambert and returned her gaze to Goddie.

Mumma went back to lie down in the bed. Goddie was devoid of thought and absent of wonder.

She quickly cleaned up the room, wiped down Mumma once again, and took the dirty laundry outside. As she rose to walk out, Lauretta stepped directly in front of her. Lauretta's grief was etched on her face. Goddie would wallow not. She picked up her belongings, squeezed past her siblings, and left.

On her way out the back door, Goddie stopped and looked back, scanning the house from left to right. She took in the untidiness, the disorganization, and the empty cupboards.

She resolved within herself that she would be much stronger, that she'd be much wiser. Surely this couldn't be all. There had to be more to this life than to live, die, and grieve. Resilience rose in her. For Goddie, it was an unacceptable notion to believe that when one dies, all must die.

*Daadie, I will not wallow in this season of grief. I must search and find a way to begin again. I need your strength to stand and move forward. I cannot count on anyone here anymore. I need you, Daadie. I need you.*

Goddie stepped off the back porch and into the rain. She had had enough.

## CHAPTER 15

# DEATH AND THE GREEN DRESS

—

The weeks following Christmas 1945 proved more exciting than the holidays themselves. Daadie had only been gone six months, but to Goddie, it felt like six days.

Mumma's grief weighed heavy on any level of festivity. Everyone came together to celebrate with feast, fellowship, and family—every family except the Ormsby's. The stench of death and long-suffering hung in the air like an unwanted guest. No one wanted to appear as if they were forgetting Daadie.

Lambert and Lincoln continued to do their best running the farm and ensured that sugar cane and coffee went to market. But times in Jamaica were changing, and the price for sugar was dropping, which impacted the family's income.

The family wasn't making enough money to support themselves. The brothers sat on the veranda for hours arguing about why they should still farm.

"I can't stay yah much longer. Dem nuh paying wi for di sugga. I can't' mek any money yah. It's time tuh head tuh Kingston now," complained Lincoln.

"If yuh think di grass sweeter, go," explained Lambert. "In da meantime, shut unnu mout. Di little ones dem still a watch wi."

Lincoln's obligations to the family held him back, and he was angry.

Lauretta was still around the house, but she had a new group of friends who loved to hang out at the Colongolook River. She didn't keep to her responsibilities, which caused great animosity among the brothers.

No one was taking care of Mumma. Although Mumma managed to make it out of her room, her depression was such that she was incapable of functioning.

Goddie didn't care about all that. She didn't care this week.

She came bounding through the door from school with her friend Ann, their eyes bright with excitement. Ann was Goddie's classmate, and the two became close soon after Daadie's funeral.

Goddie liked her because she was smart and didn't take any mess from the boys. She had been a friend in the past and proved to be her only friend in recent days.

As Goddie came through the doorway, she threw her school bag to the left and made her way past Minnette and Reynold into her room.

"Whut a gwaan, Minnette?" Goddie exclaimed as she bounded past her younger sister peeling yams. Lassie got off her seat and followed them into the room.

"Not much," replied Minnette.

"Afternoon, Lauretta," Ann squeaked out as she kept pace with Goddie. The creaky floor told everybody where they were inside Goddie's room.

She had been waiting a few days since her birthday to open a belated gift from Lauretta and Lambert. She asked them for a new dress for church. It looked like they had come through for her.

She had been thinking about putting on this dress all day. Ann helped Goddie tear open the box and rip the ribbon in excitement. They squealed as Goddie eased off the cover and parted the tissue to reveal the prize.

"Duh yuh see it? Whut ah sight! Watch ah dress!" Goddie exclaimed.

Ann's eyes danced, "Dis a whuh yuh call ah dress!!"

It was a pastel green dress straight from the United Kingdom. It came with front pockets and a dainty waist belt. It was perfect.

Ann cleared the bed, and Goddie quickly shimmied out of her dirty school clothes and threw the dress over the top of her head. She held her hands high as she allowed the garment to roll down the side of her body and fall at attention. It was perfection.

She pulled her hands out the pockets, brushed the sides of the dress, and took a glimpse in the piece of mirror nailed to the side of the wall. It was exactly what she had wanted. She had been wearing a frumpy old dress since Daadie's funeral, and it was time to give it a rest.

"I'm wearing dis dress tuh school tomorrow fi sure," gushed Goddie.

Ann smirked. "Yes, and yuh can wear it back home when Mrs. Gabriel sends yuh back to find yuh uniform too."

As much as she wanted to wear it to school the next day, Goddie knew better. Only uniforms were allowed. So, she paraded around the house, introducing her new dress to her siblings.

"Oh, watch rusty legs! Cyant have a new dress and rusty legs," Minnette said, laughing.

With that, Goddie bounded back into her room to apply some coconut oil to her dry legs and arms. She was beyond ecstatic. This was the refresher she was looking for. It had been a long, sorrowful winter, and she was ready for the rebirth. This was the perfect way to kick it off.

By this time, Lambert and Lincoln had come to see what all the commotion was about. She showed off the dress, twirling around in the middle of the room to the delight of her siblings. Lassie wanted to come closer to see it, but she had a mango in her hand and Goddie wouldn't have it. She twirled once more before walking toward Mumma's room.

"I want to show Mumma," said Goddie.

"She's sleeping. Wait likkle bit," Lauretta explained. "It's almost time tuh wake her up for her bath an fuh dinnah. She cud see it latah."

Goddie returned to her room with her sisters and Ann in tow. As they were talking about where she could wear the dress and how nice it looked, a glass crashed in the other room.

Goddie turned around to hear what was going on. It wasn't unusual for someone to drop something, but this time it sounded different. Goddie stayed silent. She held her position and studied the sounds in the next room.

Lauretta went over to see about Mumma. The seconds felt like hours. Then it began.

"NO! NO! NO! NO! NO! Come on, Mumma!"

Goddie felt Lauretta's fear in her voice.

"Come on, Mumma! Wake up, Mumma!" cried Lauretta. "Lambert! Vurley! Lincoln! COME!"

As Lauretta cried for her brothers to come into the room, Goddie's heart sank. She slowly put the tissue back in the box. Goddie knew happiness didn't last long without a hefty price.

She kept her dress on and walked slowly across the house. Her spirit said don't rush. She assessed the commotion among her siblings and knew it would not end well.

Goddie's head passed the threshold of the door frame. Lauretta was shaking Mumma, who wasn't moving. Goddie stayed at the threshold and watched. Lauretta and Lambert tried to wake her up to no avail. As they shook the bed, the broken glass shifted position all over the floor.

Mumma had dropped the jar of juice by the side of her bed. The rest of the siblings took their positions along the side of the wall, including Goddie. Miss Eileen from next door came running in to see what all the commotion was.

Since Daadie died, the neighbors in the district had been quite attentive to the siblings.

Lambert commanded, "Guh get Uncle Monroe. GO NOW!" Vurley and Reynold took off out the back door toward their uncle's land. As the frenzy elevated, Goddie looked off to her side at Lassie.

Lassie stood behind Minnette to watch what was happening to her Mumma. She looked scared. Her eyes were as big as saucers. She stared in wonderment as the juice from the mango ran the course of the floor.

Goddie shifted her eyes back to assess the prognosis. Lauretta did her best to revive her Mumma, but Goddie already knew the verdict. There was no need to scramble. There was no need to be frantic. There was no need to rush. The verdict had been delivered.

The room went silent. Lambert stood up. Lauretta stood up.

Goddie left the threshold and walked slowly into the room. Lambert stepped back as Goddie approached the bed. She quietly stepped over the broken glass to get close. She sat on the bed next to her mother and looked at her. Mumma had been curled up on her bed for so many months Goddie forgot how long she was.

She leaned in.

"Mumma?"

Nothing.

"Mumma. It's Goddie."

Nothing.

Goddie leaned over and put her ear to Mumma's chest. She had to be sure. She listened, hoping to hear something this time. A crackle, a bump, a beat. Nothing.

Mumma was gone.

Goddie had nothing left. She stood over her mother, and the whole house erupted with grief. Death was exhausting. She looked around at the strangers. Siblings once again became strangers to her. Lassie, who had dropped her mango in the commotion, hid her face behind Minnette.

The pain in the room was thick. The finality of the last six months was here at last.

*Daadie, Mumma couldn't take it anymore. The wound was too deep. We tried our best, but we had no repair for her. I'm sorry we couldn't take care of her. What will become of us now? It's too much, Daadie. It's too much. I'm all alone now. This is just too much.*

Goddie stood up, looked at her new dress, and strangely compared it to the housedress Mumma had on. It was all representative of the last six months. Even Mumma's dress wanted to get some rest. The rips, snags, and stains told the tale of a hard life lived, but in the end, a broken heart completed her story.

Goddie walked slowly toward the door. She squeezed past her siblings and through the gathering crowd of neighbors. Word had traveled that Miss Caroline was gone.

A crowd gathered in front of the house to lend support. Goddie walked past the bewildered looks of the spectators and made her way off the front steps and around the house. She sat under the tree near the outdoor kitchen. She could see the residents running toward the house.

As word spread throughout the district, it all became a strange theatre for her. She had seen all this before. She had already dreamed this. She knew it was coming.

*Daadie, where do I go from here? How will I start again?*

Daadie was gone. Mumma was gone. She would have to start over.

As was the custom, a few days later, the family held the nine-night celebration again. They had become professionals at the ceremony now.

Once again, the siblings made the slow march down the hill to the Birnhamwood church cemetery. God was merciful as the weather proved better than the last time.

There was no rain, but the wind was strong, tossing hair bonnets and dresses to and fro. Everyone wore black or dark colors except Goddie. Not today. She put on her green dress and brushed off the sides of the thighs.

She walked along with her brothers and sisters, holding Lassie's hand once again. Goddie acknowledged the villagers as she walked down the hill. Again, as they got to the church gate, they made the left toward the cemetery.

The moment compounded upon itself. This was too much for one person to bear. This was too much for one family to bear. Once again, they approached the black mango tree where they had laid their father just a few months ago.

Once again, Uncle Monroe drove the truck carrying Mumma down into the churchyard and got her close enough so the brothers could carry her off. Once again, another wood box with nails and hinges captured Goddie's attention.

They moved Mumma to the side of the plot while Ms. Eileen sang a few hymns and read a few scriptures. Goddie stood in a daze. She had foreseen this long before the moment. She was devoid of emotion and bankrupt of tears.

As the elders lowered Mumma into the ground, the eruption of grief continued. Lauretta and Lambert were inconsolable. Lincoln and Vurley stood with their heads down as tears stained their shirts. Minnette wiped the stream of tears on her face and wrapped her arms around Lassie and Reynold.

The number of mourners from up the hill was less than the mourners at Daadie's funeral. The church elders could not fill the burial plot, as the dirt was too much to lift. It was left to Lambert, Lincoln, Vurley, and Reynold to finish the task. They took turns shoveling the dirt over Mumma while the hymns pierced the afternoon sky.

The morning sun was bright, but a cool breeze had picked up from the west and carried itself through Spring Hill. As the dirt pile wound its way down, Lassie pulled on Minnette's dress. "I'm cold, Minnette." Lassie tucked herself under Minnette's arm as her big sister wrapped the other arm around Dearis.

"We have fi tek care of one another now," Minnette whispered. "We 'ave no more parents. Just us now. We 'ave no more parents."

The Ormsby children turned and began the trek through the churchyard toward the gate. Once again, Uncle Monroe was waiting with the truck outside the gate to take the family back up the hill. After a while, the Ormsby boys made their way back to the truck. The January wind had cooled off and offered no solace, not even for orphaned children.

"It a get cold out yah. Yuh not coming home?" asked Lambert as he put down the shovel and passed Goddie down the hill.

Goddie stared at the pile of dirt covering her mother. "Nuh mi fine. Mi ah go stand here for a while. I'll walk back up di hill."

Lambert looked at the waiting truck and looked back at Goddie. "Yuh sure? Mi can wait fi yuh."

"Gwaan Lambert. Mi just want tuh spend ah lickkle time."

Goddie watched as Lambert loaded up on the truck and Uncle Monroe disappeared around the bend. She turned her attention back to the place where both her parents now lay. The church was silent. The sound of children playing in the river could be heard but not much else.

The freshly dug soil stained her church shoes. She didn't care. She just wanted to be close to her parents for a little while. She took her position and slid down the trunk of the black mango tree.

She sat there alone as the sun progressed along the afternoon sky. She looked up to acknowledge the trees of Spring Hill as they stood to watch.

She watched the elders lock up the church building, and the deaconesses sweep the surrounding areas of the yard. They leaned the brooms against the building before making their way toward the church gate. They looked back and waved. Goddie waved back.

The last elder, George McIntosh, walked toward Goddie and said, "Mi very sorry 'bout unnu Mumma. She was a very good woman. She was always very kind to me. I will miss her."

"Yuh ok up here, Goddie? Want mi fi stay wid yuh?" he asked.

"It's ok, Brother McIntosh. I just want to stay wid mi parents for a likkle while."

Brother McIntosh made his way back down the hill and toward the church gate. He turned back to look at Goddie, and she waved him on. With that, he made his way to the main road.

Goddie sat and stared at the two piles of dirt. The two piles used to be people. The two piles used to be her parents. As she watched the smaller rocks roll down the mound, a tear rolled down her face.

One minute she was cooking with Daadie. The next minute he was gone. One minute she was helping Mumma in the kitchen. The next minute she was gone. All she had left was a house full of strangers.

She heaved a heavy sigh and buried her face in her hands. The two people who understood her, encouraged her, and guided her were now in the ground.

She was scared for herself and her siblings. She adjusted her position on the ground. Her new green dress was of no consequence now. She could get another dress. She couldn't get new parents. She wrapped her long arms around her knees and buried her face.

*Daadie and Mumma, the safest place is right here with you. Here, there is no need for answers. Even in death, your quiet brings me the truest peace. You protect me. Daadie, I'm sorry you died like that. You deserved better. Mumma, you have Daadie back now. I'm sorry this hurt you so. I know Daadie leaving broke your heart. I cast my lot against the world and pray. I just pray I won't be scared all the time. Cover me.*

When Goddie awoke, the sun had traced its final steps in the Spring Hill sky. Wiping the spittle off her cheek, she rose off the black mango tree, brushed the front of her dress, and walked past her parents toward the church gate.

With each step, the guilt of leaving heaved heavy on her. The tears of shame ran fast and stained her new green dress. When she reached the gate, she turned back. She wailed at the reality. Her gasps for air could not keep up with her grief. All she had left was a wave.

"Goodbye, Daadie. Goodbye, Mumma. I will love you forever. Thank you," she whispered.

She pressed away from the gate post and walked toward the setting sun.

Goddie was an orphan.

# PART IV

# PSALM 55

## CHAPTER 16

# PSALM 55

---

The morning breeze came in and circulated Goddie's room before exploring the rest of the house. She had graduated to Daadie's side of the bed along with Lauretta.

One of the small mercies in Mumma's death was the opportunity to spread out the sleeping arrangements. The room was simple but reverent. A simple wood bed frame, washbasin, and rocking chair made up most of the furnishings, and Goddie could look at the window from her side of the mattress. Her parents worked their whole lives, yet their possessions could be accounted for in a glance.

The days of waking up to Minnette's snoring and Dearis' foot in Goddie's back were over. Goddie stretched her legs out past her bedsheet. Growing up meant just that and being able to stretch out on a bed was a luxury. Lauretta was careful to keep the simple room spotless.

The spring months had been relatively quiet and mostly uneventful in the district. It had been several months since the burial of Mumma, and Goddie was finally able to rest.

*Well, hello there,* she thought to herself as she wiggled her toes back and forth. She raised her foot and rotated her ankles as her body came alive to greet the day.

No more feet hanging off the side of the bed. Goddie was changing. She was maturing. She examined her wrists and fingernails. She admired the extension of her forearms. She was growing from a young girl to a young lady. In another year, she would be an adult.

She stared up at the tin roof and thought about the future. She only had another few years to finish her secondary education, but her mind was always on the next thing. James taught her to think that way. Always be looking forward.

Like any teenager, she relished the chance to just stay in bed. Saturday morning meant no rush for school and no rush for morning chores. For now, her joy was as simple as rotating her wrists in the air and celebrating momentary laziness in the district of Spring Hill.

Her view from the new bedroom faced the other side of the house and, with that, a different perspective.

The sounds of children at the river were clear, and the banter of chickens outside could interrupt any daydream. Goddie looked around the room that used to belong to her parents.

Daadie's boots were still in the corner from the day he died. They served as a monument to him, and no one dared disturb them. Mumma's apron hung on the nail in the wall. On Goddie's side of the bed lay Daadie's Bible. It was a thick King James Version that had been passed down for generations.

Goddie only saw Daadie's Bible in one of two places. Either it was in Daadie's hands or on the side of his bed. She remembered how he always used a grass blade to mark his favorite verses.

Daadie was their first bishop, and the family loved him for that. He didn't have a formal education, but he chronicled the family tree like a genealogist. Every birth, death, and marriage was cataloged within the first few pages of his Bible. He noted every relative, all their children, and any special things to know. There were even a few names of people he wasn't related to.

The pages bristled with every turn, but the knowledge Daadie collected stayed true. The bound leather cover was dry and worn, but he was careful to rub a little oil on it every now and then. His treasured passages were not hard to identify, as the well-worn spine gave away every secret location.

Goddie sat up in bed and reached for the thick book. She could not help but notice two praying mantises fighting on the windowsill on her side of the bed. She placed her bets on the one on the left.

"Daadie used to call those God Horses," she said and smirked. She gazed long enough to watch the mantis on the right finally succumb and fall off the sill.

"Yuh wretch yuh," whispered Goddie as she turned her attention back to Daadie's Bible. With two hands, she heaved the thick book into her lap. She flipped to one of the locations where Daadie had placed a fresh piece of grass.

*Psalm 55, huh? Well, let's see what yuh have to say,* she thought.

*For it was not an enemy that reproached me; then I could have borne it: neither was it he that hated me that did magnify himself against me; then I would have hid myself from him:*

*But it was thou, a man mine equal, my guide, and mine acquaintance.*

*We took sweet counsel together, and walked unto the house of God in company.*

*(King James Bible, Psalm 55:12-14)*

Goddie reflected a moment and closed Daadie's Bible. Her thoughts were soon broken by the sounds of arguing coming from just outside the window. Lambert and Lauretta were going at each other in front of the house, and Goddie could only hear fragments of the conversation.

Then she heard her name. She leaned in closer only to hear her name again.

"If we don't come up with the school fee, Goddie will have to leave school. This isn't me. This is the headmaster," explained Lambert.

"So, our family is the only family that nuh have school fee? Is who yuh tryin' to tell this to? Me?" replied Lauretta.

Goddie gently placed Daadie's Bible back on the nightstand and moved off the bed. She crept slowly up to the window. From the back window, she couldn't see who was talking, but she could hear them loud and clear. She rested her arms on the sill and waited for the next exchange.

"Lower yuh voice. They might hear us," whispered Lambert. He cleared his throat and continued. "This may be the only option. All the other school fees are much cheaper, as the others are in lower levels. The price we are getting for sugar cannot support Goddie's' school fee any longer. We don't have it. Cane and coffee nuh selling at high prices, and the traders have options. Mexico ah sell banana fe half of what we sell. We are at the mercy of the market price. If they can buy cheaper, they will buy cheaper. Right now, they can buy cheaper," Lambert explained.

"So…we are to send Goddie away to live with Mrs. Sulkett so she can help with her mother? What happens to Goddie's schooling?" lamented Lauretta.

Goddie leaned farther over the sill. She could hear her sister starting to cry.

"Mrs. Sulkett will pay for the schooling. Goddie just has to look after her mother when she's not in school."

"I don't know Lambert. I don't know. "

"If we don't pay the fee, Goddie nah go ah school. We don't have the fee," explained Lambert.

"So, who to tell 'ar?" questioned Lauretta.

"Tell me what?" demanded Goddie from the porch. She gave up spying at the window and came out front.

The siblings looked at each other like strangers.

Lincoln came out of the house and stood on the porch as Goddie stepped down and walked toward her brother and sister. She tightened her fists as she pounded the ground in their direction. Lambert and Lauretta looked at each other and then back at Goddie. Lincoln went back inside to get the rest of the family. Before long, the entire Ormsby clan was outside on the porch awaiting the response to Goddie's question.

Lambert started, "We are running out of money, Goddie. We can't afford your schooling. So…"

"So yuh trading me off like a goat to a stranger to make unnu life easier," finished Goddie. She stared straight at Lauretta. Lauretta cast her eyes to the ground.

"If yuh can trade me off, Lauretta, yuh can look at me," commanded Goddie as the tears welled. Lauretta stepped back behind Lambert as she tried to hide her tears.

Goddie's chest heaved for air. "Am I not worth fighting for? AM I NOT WORTH FIGHTING FOR? AM I NOT?"

She looked up into the sky.

*Yuh see what you left here, Daadie? It hasn't even been a year and the family mashup already.*

Goddie looked back to see the remaining siblings. She scanned their faces from left to right. With one look, it all became clear. There was her, and there was them. She was no longer a part of them. She was the hinge, and the hinge was now broken.

Goddie always knew she was the bridge that connected the oldest four siblings with the youngest four siblings. For her entire life, she was the interpreter for the baby siblings and the defender to her older ones. She took care of them when they were sick. She made sure they were ready for school. She walked them to school. She covered them while they slept. Goddie was the surrogate.

The sound of the goats broke the silence. She trained her eyes back on her older siblings. "Even the goats get to stay," she sobbed. "Who have yuh sold me off to?"

"Her name is Mrs. Sulkett. She's from Spring Hill. She needs help taking care of her mother. Yuh are going to help her, and she will pay for yuh schooling. This is the best thing for you. I've made the decision," explained Lambert.

Goddie tilted her head to the side. "You've made the decision? If it's the best thing, why don't you go? Don't jook out my eye and tell me I look good with one," she replied as she wiped her eyes with her housedress. Goddie grew impatient with the moment.

"Even Joseph's brothers knew to sell him for twenty pieces of silver. So did Judas. Yuh just gave me away. An ox would get more," she screamed.

Lambert looked up from the ground and locked eyes with her. She was right, and he knew it. So did Lauretta.

Goddie caught her breath, wiped her tears with her house-dress, and turned back toward the house. King Lambert had already decided. After a few steps, Goddie turned around.

"Where in Spring Hill does she live?"

"Broadgate."

Lauretta's eyes got big as she walked around to face Lambert. "Broadgate? You told me she was from Spring Hill? Broadgate is in St. Mary Parish, not Portland! That's over twenty-five miles from here! What did you do, Lambert?" she screamed, pounding his chest.

Lambert pushed her to the side and cleared his throat. "She is from Spring Hill. She now lives in Broadgate. She will be here in a few days to get you." With that, he turned and walked toward the open field.

"But we will never see her. We can barely get crops to market now. How are we going to get to Broadgate, Lambert?" Lincoln shouted. Lambert kept walking.

"So…we won't see Goddie again?" asked Reynold with tears in his eyes.

"No. Lambert and Lauretta are sending her away," responded Dearis.

The veranda erupted at the realization that in a few days, Goddie would not be living with them anymore. She would be sent away to live with strangers to work for her education.

The baby siblings held each other in agony as Lauretta dropped to the ground in grief. Once again, wailing was the hymn that rose from the Ormsby farm. In less than one year, the family would be forced to grieve three times.

Goddie stopped mid-stride and turned to face her older siblings.

"Yuh think yuh are Daadie. Yuh are no Daadie. He would have nevah done this. This ditch yuh dig for me, yuh better dig two for you," Goddie said, sobbing. She changed course and walked around the house and down the path.

"Where are yuh going?" cried Minnette.

"To be with the real Daadie."

The siblings cried as they watched Goddie disappear around the corner.

## CHAPTER 17

# LAST MORNING

———

The door to the bedroom slowly creaked open. Whatever the door hinges failed to announce, the floorboards made up for. Minnette whispered, "Goddie. Wake up. Goddie, time tuh wake up. Wake up nuh? They are outside waiting." She stood waiting for her sister to move, but it was of no use.

It was Goddie's last day in Spring Hill. Only a few days earlier, Lambert had told her she would be living with strangers. She had spent most of those days in her parent's bed, taking in her surroundings as much as possible. Her friend Ann had come over a few times to sit with her, but Goddie elected to journey these final moments alone.

Anger consumed her. It consumed every act of cogitation. Goddie was in no hurry to leave her home, her land, and her parents.

She clenched her jaw and didn't move an inch. She tucked her nightdress around her body tightly so they would not have anything to grip. This day was hers. Lambert had already sold off the rest of her days. He couldn't have this one, and she didn't care who was outside.

Lying on her parent's bed was the last goodbye she cared about, and it would not be rushed. She could feel Minnette bending over and cupping her hands around Goddie's ear.

"If yuh holler in mi ear again, I will box yuh," warned Goddie. "Mek dem wait. It may be di first an' last time dem wait on mi. Why should I be inna hurry to be a slave? If dem nuh like it, Jamaica is a free country," declared Goddie.

She pulled the sheet away from Minnette's grip and turned over. As she pulled the sheet over her head, she knew there was no escaping this day. The room was silent. She created a peek hole in the sheet and opened one eye to see where Minnette was.

The traitors, dressed as siblings, surrounded Mumma's bed staring at her. She registered their faces one by one— Lauretta, Lincoln, Vurley, Dearis, Reynold, and Minnette. She looked around for Lassie and finally found her standing in the corner by Daadie's boots.

"All yuh missing now is the executioner. Where is he?" she snarked as she closed the peephole back over her eyes.

"Lambert is outside talking to Mrs. Sulkett and fe 'ar daughters dem," responded Lauretta. "It's time tuh put yuh tings together. Rain is coming and they came in an open truck. Di driver nuh waan di rain fe ketch him."

"Jamaica is a free country. Nobody nah stop him," said Goddie.

Goddie could hear their sniffling from underneath the covers. Their tears were of no consequence to her. She blamed everyone in the house. Those able and those not able to stop this horse trade.

She knew everyone stood to benefit from her absence. There would be more money for everyone, more beds for everyone, and more food for everyone. Even Lassie would now get a space on the bed.

Goddie heard Lambert's stride as the pounding came closer and closer. The shadow of his presence darkened the morning light from the window. She opened her eyes to the shadow and pulled the sheet from up over her head. Goddie opened her eyes slowly and looked straight at her older brother.

She wasn't afraid of him. Whatever respect she had left for him would stay in Mumma's room long after she climbed onto that truck. Lambert's face was angry, but his eyes were despondent. He had to keep to the arrangement, but his eyes knew this could be different. It was too late now. The horse was out of the gate.

"I see the executioner has arrived. Are yuh ready to trade me now, sire?" asked Goddie. She looked him straight in the eye without blinking.

Lambert looked back at this sister. "Dem a wait pon yuh. The truck is loaded. It's time now. Dem leaving within di hour."

"Dem can cut out now. It wud badda mi none at all," said Goddie.

"Try and look at dis different Goddie. Yuh a di brightest one ah wi all. I nevah want tuh risk yuh education. I know dis nuh feel good right now but dis a di best move. Dem promise tuh keep yuh in school," explained Lambert.

"Trading mi like ah donkey a di bess move? A promise is a comfort to a fool, Lambert. Today, yuh a di fool." Goddie said as she flung the bedsheet off her body.

"Get out so I can get ready to be traded. Tell my new owners I will be ready widin di hour. Get out."

All the siblings turned to leave Mumma's room. As Goddie watched the back of Lambert leave, she swung her feet over the side of the wooden bed. She walked over to the window and rested her arms on the sill for the last time.

She took a deep breath, held it, and exhaled slowly. Goddie tried to pack her lungs with as much of the morning breeze as possible. Tomorrow, the breeze would blow differently. She inhaled again, slowly closing her eyes and holding her breath.

*Daadie, you and Mumma see and know what is going on here. They are sending me away. Just me. Only me. It hurts, Daadie. Why me? I start this new life without parents and without siblings. I start this new life without friends and without enemies.*

*I start this new life alone. Just me one. Everything is dark around me. Everything is strange around me. I'm afraid. I can't let them know, but Daadie, yuh know. Cover me, Daadie. Protect me, Mumma.*

When she opened her eyes, Lassie was still in the corner by Daadie's boots. Her baby sister was frozen. Whatever the breakfast was, Lassie had it all over her face and clothes—the stain of morning tea around her cheeks now mixed with tears and mucous as she tucked herself in the corner of the room unnoticed.

Goddie sat back on the bed and called her over. Lassie pushed off the wall and made her way over to her sister's bedside. Goddie put her arm around Lassie, and Lassie wrapped her tiny arm around Goddie's waist. She nuzzled her face into her sister's side, and the two Ormsby girls sobbed in agreement as they stared out the window.

Lassie was too young to understand, and Goddie was too confused to explain. They only had a consensus on the pain. It was possible they would never see each other again. The realization was too heavy for words to yield the matter.

"Hush, it will be ok, Lassie. God watching all a wi. When I am far, remember he is near. 'member ok? We will be together again. Where I am, yuh will be too. Me nah forget yuh baby."

Lassie looked up. "Ok."

Goddie wiped off her baby sister's face with her house-dress. She tidied up the braid that had come loose in the back of Lassie's head and cleaned out her eyes.

"Buck up, mon. Goddie loves you." She gave her a squeeze, and Lassie looked up and gave her a wink with both eyes. The two chuckled in the light moment.

"Now go wash-up. Mi nuh want no dutty face goodbye."

With that, Lassie jumped off the bed and trotted out of the room.

# CHAPTER 18

# GOODBYE, SPRING HILL

———

Goddie stood in the middle of the house. With everyone outside, all was quiet.

The smell of dumplings and salt-fish was nowhere to be found. The busyness of the district outside kept their commotion to a small roar. There were no sounds of children playing in the Colongolook River. The mothers weren't gossiping, and the merchants traded in silence. The postman dropped his obligations and forewent the usual chat with the district villagers. The yard dogs elected to sprawl out on the veranda and stayed out of the way.

Somehow, it seemed like the district of Spring Hill knew she was leaving.

She ran her hand along the walls and smelled the drapes. She sat for a moment on Mumma's old chair before walking out back to the kitchen. She plucked a few bush leaves Mumma used to make tea with and shoved them in her pocket. As she made her way back inside, she grabbed the wooden ladle Mumma used to make soup.

"Yuh coming with me," she whispered as she shoved the long wooden spoon in a pillowcase.

Daadie hadn't built a mansion, but it was theirs and it was home. She was born in that house. She was raised in that house. She was loved in that house.

She straightened a few things for the last time and brushed off the front of her dress. She almost made it past the threshold when she remembered the most important thing.

"I almost forgot," she whispered as she turned around in mid-step. She shuffled back into Mumma's room and walked around to Daadie's side of the bed.

"Yuh coming with me too," Goddie muttered as she picked up Daadie's Bible and stuffed the behemoth book into the pillowcase. She covered up the treasure with her shawl and made her way out the door. As she walked through the threshold, she caught Reynold crying in the corner on the veranda.

He looked up and wiped his eyes. "So yuh really leaving me, Goddie? Will I see yuh again?"

Goddie stared at him and then looked beyond him to the truck with strangers waiting to whisk her away. She bent down and rubbed his head. She reached under and cupped his face in her hands. Her eyes welled up again with tears.

"I don't know when I'll see yuh. But as soon as I can, I'll be back. Yuh 'ave to take care of Lassie now. Duh yuh think yuh can duh that? She's going to need yuh now."

He nodded.

Goddie kissed Reynold's forehead and stood up. She reached out her hand. "Yuh want tuh see me off?"

He wiped his nose and nodded his head.

"Ok, let's go."

Goddie and her brother walked across the yard together toward Lambert, Lauretta, and a group of strangers. Two small trucks were parked outside the house.

"I'm ready, Lambert," she announced.

Goddie made eye contact with a short dumpy woman in a dress. Her presence commanded attention, but there wasn't much to her. She was quite plain. Beside her were three young girls about Goddie's age who glanced upward at her presence.

The woman stepped forward with an outstretched hand.

"I'm Mrs. Sulkett. You can call me Mumma Sulkett."

"I only 'ave one Mumma. She's gone now," replied Goddie.

"Very well. We'll figure it out. These are my daughters Vera, Ina, and Ruth. We are so very happy yuh agreed to come to live wid us. We have a long journey ahead, so we should be going before the rain starts. We don't have protection with the open truck, so we should go. The drivers are ready."

With that, she climbed into the front seat of the truck with one of her daughters in tow. One of the trucks was already loaded up with vegetables, and the back of the other appeared empty. Lincoln and Vurley loaded the last of Goddie's belongings into the bed of the second truck and stepped back.

The crack of thunder broke the morning tension. The Ormsby siblings lined up in a row to say goodbye, but Goddie walked directly over to Lambert and Lauretta.

"Explain tuh mi how ah woman wid three daughters mi age needs help tuh tek care of her Mumma? Explain that."

Lambert gazed straight ahead. Goddie never broke her stare. Lambert never broke his gaze as a tear ran down his cheek.

She reached around to hug her big brother and pulled him close. He pushed back on the hug, but her grip would not be denied. She reached out and dragged Lauretta in.

"As God know, mark this day. I will nevah forgive yuh for sending me away. Yuh dug my ditch, but yuh just dug two fuh you." She kissed her oldest siblings on the cheek and continued down the line to say goodbye to the others.

"Lincoln, be sure to help with the farm."

"Vurley, I'll miss yuh. Keep an eye on Reynold."

"Minnette and Dearis, look after Lassie."

"Reynold, study yuh book and listen to Vurley now."

The youngest boy nodded in agreement.

Her final goodbye was saved for the baby. She reached down and picked her up in the air. Lassie squeezed her sister's neck tightly as her feet dangled. Goddie could feel the tears and mucus on the side of her neck.

"Yuh be a nice gyal now 'ear? Soon come back," she whispered. "Be brave. Goddie love you."

Another thunder crack in the sky signaled the end of the long goodbye. Goddie walked to the side of the second truck to climb in. She grabbed the door handle, but the door was locked. She looked up to lock eyes with Vera.

"We 'ave nuh room up front. Climb in di back an' mek wi go. Di rain soon ketch wi," Mrs. Sulkett commanded from the other truck.

"Di rain soon ketch yuh," chimed Vera as the sisters giggled to themselves. They made no room inside for Goddie.

Goddie climbed into the back of the open truck and braced herself for the twenty-five-mile journey down the mountain. She grabbed the edge of the truck bed with one hand and the pillowcase with Daadie's Bible with the other.

As the second truck shifted gears, she locked her eyes on Lambert and Lauretta. Her soul stared into the soul of the traders who had sent her away.

The sky finally exploded, revealing the Lord's displeasure. The lightning lit the way, and the rain became incessant. Goddie kept her eyes on her siblings until they disappeared around the corner. The sheets of rain hit Goddie's face in mercy.

As the trucks pulled onto the main road, a familiar face stood under the tree. Goddie cupped her hands around her eyes to see the stranger better. It was James. There he was, soaked to the skin, waiting on his schoolmate and friend to pass by.

The sadness surrounding him cut through the storm. Goddie sat up taller to see him better. He walked out from under the canopy and waved with both hands as the truck descended down the hill.

James's voice cut through the torrential as he shouted, "Bye, Goddie! Miss yuh."

"Bye, Ja......"

A bump in the road mercifully forced her further back into the truck. She didn't want him to see her tears.

The final curve in the hill was the greatest heartbreak. She sat up straight and craned her neck to catch a final glimpse of the churchyard where her parents were buried.

She knew Mrs. Sulkett wouldn't dare stop the trucks, so Goddie positioned herself to fill her eyes with as much as possible. First, she saw the churchyard gate, then the top of the church, then there it was the two mounds of dirt under the black mango tree were visible for a few moments before the brush took over.

"Bye, Daadie. Bye, Mumma. Bye, Da..." She could barely get the words out before the winds threw her to the back of the truck-bed.

They continued north as the winds beat the sides of the open truck and the rain hammered Goddie.

Goddie cast a despondent gaze as she watched the only place she had ever known disappear in front of her. Each turn compounded the goodbye, each gear change a reminder that getting back to Spring Hill would likely never happen.

She looked off into the distance as the trees of Spring Hill waved goodbye. She waved back. The canopies moved in unison as the winds dictated their dance. Goddie was reduced to waving her fingers.

She was wet and tired. The rain drummed her body into submission as her belongings lay soaked in the back of the truck. She reached over to check Daadie's Bible in the pillowcase. The Bible was dry. She sat there confused at the fact. Everything in the truck was soaked, including her. The Bible was dry.

She sat there for a second more, and a big smile came over her. It was a sign.

"Thank you, Daadie." She chuckled before she threw another covering over the pillowcase. After a while, the rain relented, the roads smoothed out, and evening sun trailed behind the truck.

Goddie fell asleep.

# CHAPTER 19

# NOT FRIENDS

———

Goddie held her weathered hands against the bottle torchlight. She ran her fingers over the cracks of her hands and feet. She had only left Spring Hill a few months ago, but her hands told the story of a girl sentenced to hard labor in the salt mines.

She summoned her last remnant of strength to slip out of her work dress and flop on her bed, even though the straw sack Mrs. Sulkett called a bed offered no respite to an aching body.

The steady drone of rain seeped through the holes of the aluminum roof and forced her to drag the dingy sack bed to the corner of the room. The disrepair of the shanty back room would aggravate the most hardened prisoner, let alone a young girl.

The arrangement made by Lambert and Lauretta was a promise to a fool. What fools they were. Goddie suffered weeks of loneliness and heartache as she took on caring for Mrs. Sulkett's mother, Ms. Maude.

Her insufferable nature was only made more potent by her inability to care for herself even slightly. Whatever failings she had in life were now the albatross she carried into old age. Goddie wasn't surprised when she learned Ms. Maude had run off four other caregivers in the last two years.

Goddie's days under Mrs. Sulkett were difficult. Day after day, she slaved to take care of five females quite able to take care of themselves. She was subject to every stupid whim of her overseer and every maniacal need of her daughters.

Taking care of Ms. Maude was the hardest thing she had ever done. It was backbreaking. Goddie drifted between sunrise and sunset with only the hardness of her hands to remind her of what once was.

Her thoughts of the future were bartered for thoughts of laundry, cleaning the house, repairing clothes, and washing the incessant grime off an old lady. After a few months, Goddie knew this house was the place where spirits were vanquished, and souls disappeared.

She turned her head toward the wall. Above her hung the birthday dress from Lambert and Lauretta. It had been months since she felt like a young lady. She reached up and ran her fingers along the hem of the dress. The tears that fell couldn't decide if they were for what was or what is now. Perhaps it was both.

*Daadie, how could I have fallen so far? This measure of life is undeserved and without end. My life has been disturbed. My light has been obscured. My strength has been ransomed. My only desir....*

"Yuh finish tek out the hem for Miss Rickett?" asked Mrs. Sulkett as she swung open the door.

"No, ma'am. I 'ave to finish mi homework first," Goddie replied.

"Oh no! How yuh tink yuh school fees paid? Prayers and buttons?

"I was late for school dis mawning again because of all the tings yuh have me doing from sunrise. It's too much work. I keep missing the school truck and have to walk to school. It's a four-mile walk," complained Goddie.

"It could be ten miles mi nuh care. Finish whuh mi tell yuh tuh finish."

It was clear who held the handle and who held the blade. Goddie stared right through her.

"Yuh bettah finish all dis hem repair BEFORE yuh finish yuh schoolwork. Nuh mek mi come back in yah," she snorted and slammed the back room door.

"That ole bitch," Goddie muttered.

Goddie had been keeping count. Tomorrow would make the sixth day in three weeks she was late for school. The headmaster had already warned her that any more tardiness would result in a failing grade. Her grades had declined since coming to St. Mary's Parish, and making friends seemed impossible.

She found it impossible to repair clothes, fetch water, and move the goats all before the school truck left in the morning for Castleton Secondary School.

Mrs. Sulkett didn't care. She had a personal handmaid now, and she was riding this horse until it fell over or ran away.

Goddie grabbed the skirt for Miss Rickett and started taking out the hem. It was an old housedress with big pockets in the front. She stared at them for a long time. Mumma had the same housedress with the same big pockets.

She started taking out the hem and thinking about her siblings. Her anger toward Lambert and Lauretta never subsided. The heartbreak was as raw as her hands. It had been months since she saw Lassie's toothless grin. She missed Minnette's foot in her back in the early morning, and she even missed Lincoln's voice in the field. Loneliness was a curse, and she lived it every day.

The back room where Goddie had lived had a small window that opened to the field. The luxury of leaning on the sill to daydream was left in Spring Hill. Now the window was a highway for flies and mosquitoes in the hot summer months.

Everything that was once lovely in Spring Hill was now cursed. She had no family, no friends, and no freedom. The summer rain drummed the song of freedom on the roof—freedom for everyone but her. There would be no morning breeze in Broadgate. There was no breeze at all.

"Knock, knock."

Goddie didn't respond. If she didn't have freedom over her education, she certainly didn't have freedom over a door in a house. She waited while she picked apart the hem.

"Knock, knock." The door opened slightly. "Goddie?"

"Who is there?" muttered Goddie.

"Vera. May I come in?"

Goddie's disgust for Mrs. Sulkett extended to everyone and everything connected to her, including her daughters. Making time to play nice when she had a pile of clothes to repair, and incomplete homework seemed stupid to her. Goddie repositioned herself on the straw sack bed.

"It's your house. I can't stop yuh," replied Goddie.

Vera slowly opened the door wide enough to stick her head in. Of all the siblings, she'd proven to be the most kind since Goddie's arrival. Vera was a simple soul with not much to her. She was short and dumpy like her mother, but she had a level of intellect that allowed Goddie to tolerate her moderately.

Vera sauntered up to Goddie and plopped down on the pile of clothes. "Do yuh like it here, Goddie?" she asked.

"Sure, living here sewing clothes fuh strangers is every-thing I ever dreamed of," responded Goddie. She barely lifted her head to acknowledge her unwelcomed guest. "If yuh mother wonders why those clothes are crushed up, I'm going to tell her it's yuh. Yuh either get off the clothes or press them."

Vera readjusted her seat and stared at Goddie. Goddie lifted her head to stare right back at her.

"Whuh yuh want, Vera? Yuh and mi are not friends. I am the servant and yuh are the owner's daughter. Let's not pretend and play dolly house. I'm tired and I have work to do. Apparently, my school fees depend on it," snarked Goddie. "Either yuh help or yuh get out. I prefer yuh just get out."

Vera stayed on the bed, looking off into the corner of the room. Her gaze suggested something was wrong, but Goddie didn't have the luxury or the time to pay attention to anything that wouldn't pay her school fees. She wasn't concerned about Vera's horrible days. They didn't measure to Goddie's horrible life.

The awkward silence was only broken by the rain beating the aluminum roof in the back. Goddie grew impatient.

"My birthday is coming up. What do you think I should do to celebrate?" asked Vera.

"My mother and father's death anniversary is coming up. What do you think I should do to celebrate? replied Goddie as she looked Vera square in the face with all the contempt she could muster.

Goddie straightened her back and turned to Vera. "Let's get something straight. You and me? We nah friends. I am a girl who belongs to yuh mother for which she pays my school fee. I work for yuh Mumma, which means I work fi you. Let's not pretend we are friends unless yuh taking some of this work off me. I 'ave siblings. I 'ave eight of them that I haven't seen in months. They have all but forgotten me by now. No letters. No visits. No thoughts. No prayers. You in my room is a reminder that I left my mother's soft bed fi dis straw bag, and I 'ave more work than the mule out front.

Suh, please, nuh baddah wid the nice talk. Either help or leave."

Vera looked away, dejected, she pressed off the bed to stand up.

"Sorry tuh bother yuh. I'll leave yuh alone," Vera murmured.

"Yuh should be. When I'm no longer yuh servant, yuh can be my friend. Until then, stick to business," Goddie replied as she got back to repairing the skirt hem.

As soon as Vera left, a knock from the other wall could be heard. It was the miserable Ms. Maude.

"Knock, knock."

"Goddie yuh 'dere?" Ms. Maude inquired. "I need yuh to wash me up now. Hurry up. Mi a get sleepy now."

Goddie looked out the half-opened window facing nowhere. She listened to the rain running off the roof. The sound of peace was interrupted by the squawk of a miserable brute. The sheer pitch of that voice box was enough to turn a nun violent. Her very sound was a reminder of Goddie's circumstances.

A year ago, she was a daughter. Now she was enslaved, washing clothes for some, repairing clothes for others, and cleaning a house for strangers.

Her tears flowed at the thought of her old life. Her house-dress consoled her as she wiped her face. She was much more than a promoted slave. She was the daughter of Christopher and Caroline Ormsby. The middle child of nine from the district of Spring Hill. She was more than the grime coming off an old woman's back.

As she gathered herself and wiped her tears, a wave of realization washed over her. She began to smile.

"Goddie, I'm waiting. Hurry up nuh! My body needs fi wash now," barked Ms. Maude.

Goddie straightened up and brushed the front of her dress. She grabbed the washtub from the corner and the carbolic soap on the sill. She wrung out the rag and threw a towel over her shoulder. Her smile turned into a slight chuckle.

She flung open her door and walked next door to the room of the miserable woman. Goddie's smile never faded. It got bigger.

"Wah yuh smiling 'bout?" asked Ms. Maude.

Goddie began to wash Ms. Maude's back. "Nothing. Nothing at all."

Goddie smiled at Ms. Maude, and Ms. Maude stared right back at Goddie. Goddie didn't care.

She had already decided. She was leaving.

# CHAPTER 20

# LONG WALK

———

Goddie's idea of time had become deluded and delusional. Sunrise became sunset and evening became morning without explanation. What was once normal drifted across the line to abnormal. What was once common quickly become crass and uncharacteristic.

Her life, in a few months, had spiraled from student to servant. A life once flush with friends, family, and faith now was a shadow of loneliness and despondency.

The headmaster at Castleton Secondary School warned that she would suffer severe academic consequences if she didn't improve her grades and her truancy. Both suffered miserably, and eventually, she was asked to leave the school. Now working for school fees became working for rent.

She found herself far from the dreams of her parents and the instruction of her siblings. Her year-long loathing of Lambert and Lauretta transitioned into a longing for the familiar. The months had worn down her anger, and Goddie just wanted to leave.

The memories of Goddie's friends and neighbors began to fade from her mind. There was no room and no use for romantic journeys of what was. It had been over a year since both Christopher and Caroline Ormsby took their rest, and nobody mentioned, much less cared about, Goddie's grief. Some days even Goddie forgot.

Goddie took no interest in learning the Broadgate district. She didn't care about the markets, the craftsmen, or the tradesmen. She wasn't interested in making friends, attending church, or being neighborly.

She wasn't staying. Not staying meant not making nice. Goddie no longer counted the days or change of clothes. She wore the same thing every day. The harder her hands got, the harder her heart got toward Broadgate and all who were in it.

Goddie finally cleared the window in the back room where she slept. It wasn't perfect, but she could lean on the sill, enjoy the morning breeze, and watch the chickens in the coop.

There were at least fifty chickens. The family raised chickens and sold their eggs to the local shops. Goddie watched as the hens carried on conversations among themselves. They ate the finest feed and slept on a bed much better than hers. Mrs. Sulkett had several coops, and her reputation for good eggs was known in the district.

"These damn birds eat bettah than me tuh rhaatid," cursed Goddie.

"Which damn birds?" asked Mrs. Sulkett as she revealed her eavesdropping location at the door.

Goddie snapped around and looked her straight in the eye. "Nothing, ma'am."

"Since yuh and the birds dem nah get along, I 'ave something I need you to do today. Finish get ready and meet me in front of the house. Don't be long," she said.

A few minutes later, Goddie reported out front to a waiting Mrs. Sulkett. As Goddie approached, she saw something wrapped up in cloth. It was some sort of container.

Mrs. Sulkett began the instruction. "Ok look, Goddie, I need yuh to tek dis yah package down to Ina now. She's working in Annotto Bay for the week, and she forgot to tek it wid 'ar. Mek sure yuh hold it straight and don't mek it drain out."

The package was an awkward fifteen pounds. It was double wrapped with no handles. Goddie turned it around a few times and looked up.

"How am I to hold dis, ma'am?" asked Goddie. "There are no handles."

"With yuh two hands."

"Ma'am, do yuh 'ave fare for the bus?"

Mrs. Sulkett's eyebrows raised high. "Bus? Yuh mad? Tek deh package and get going. Mek sure yuh back before sunset."

Goddie looked at the package some more and then looked down the road. Her eyes narrowed at the realization.

"Ma'am, we passed Annotto Bay the day yuh bring me 'ere. That is a six-mile walk to the north shore one way. De road dem bruk up and the trucks run fast through the narrows. That's a four-hour-plus walk by myself."

Mrs. Sulkett removed her horned-rimmed glasses and wiped her forehead with the front of her housedress. She replaced the glasses on her nose and scanned Goddie slowly from head to toe.

"Mek sure yuh come back before sunset. If yuh don't deliver the package, don't come back." She turned and walked back toward the chicken coop.

Goddie stood there for a long time, pondering the ultimatum that had no good outcome. Either walk the twelve miles round trip or suffer the wrath of the chicken coop master.

She tightened her sandals, brushed the front of her housedress off, and walked through the gate holding the package with both hands.

Goddie moved quickly along the roadside, being very careful not to walk too close to the bushes or too far out into the road. She heard Lauretta talking about young girls getting snatched up into the bushes. She wasn't interested in becoming one of those girls.

Eventually, her arms ached from carrying the package with both hands, and her feet wore raw from the fractured roads of St. Mary's Parish. As she reached the halfway mark, she stopped and rested in front of a merchant shop near the Aqua Alta River.

She had seen the river many times, as it ran straight through Broadgate. Goddie bathed in the river a few times, but the distance from the house proved troublesome just for bathing. She remembered it well, as it was easy to see the boulders sticking out of the riverbed after each storm.

She settled the package beside her and removed her sandals. Her broad feet sighed relief from the incarceration, and she wiggled her toes in the St. Mary air.

She sat and remembered when she used to walk on her hands and feet together. This caused her hands to enlarge. Even after Goddie learned to walk, she went for years without shoes. Eventually, her feet became so enlarged, finding shoes for church was difficult.

"Yuh look tired," said a strange voice behind her.

Goddie turned around to see a short Chinese man blocking the sun.

"I am John Chin. I own this store," the stranger said as he stepped away from the sun. "Yuh want a drink or something?"

"My Mumma said neveh to eat from strange people," Goddie replied. She stared for a while at the strange Chinese man. He sounded like a Jamaican, but he looked completely Chinese.

"Yuh Mumma is a wise woman," John said.

"She was a wise woman. She died over a year ago." The conversation went quiet as they both tried to figure out the best way out of the exchange.

"How far is Annotto Bay from here, sir?" Goddie asked as she rubbed her sore feet.

John rubbed his forehead. "Yuh walking there? Lawd, that's at least an hour's walk from here. Why yuh nah tek bus? It would cost yuh about one pound."

"Yuh need bus fare for bus. I don't have a pound. I better get going. Night gonna ketch me out her fuh sure if I don't hurry." Goddie put her sandals back on and grabbed the package.

John watched the young girl struggling to hold the package with two hands.

"Wait here for one second. Be right back," he said and disappeared into the store. In two minutes, he came back with a potato sack and a knife. Goddie watched as he quickly cut holes in the sack, tied the ends, and fashioned the bag into a quick satchel. He double tied the ends before he handed it to the wide-eyed girl.

"This should make the journey a bit easier. Yuh should get going before dark catch yuh," counseled the shopkeeper.

"Thank you, sir," Goddie replied. It was the first act of kindness from anybody in over a year. She positioned the package in the satchel and continued down the road, swinging her hands in relief.

"I'll be here if you need a drink on the way back. Nuh worry yuh self about the money. My treat. Be sure to stop when yuh come though," he said, waving as he stepped back into the store.

The St. Mary's sun made the trek to the north shore regretful. When she finally reached Ina, she handed her the package outside of her workplace.

"Why are you here?" Ina asked, confused. "I didn't see the bus pull up. Yuh walked 'ere, Goddie?"

Goddie stumbled over to a nearby patch of grass and plopped down. She was exhausted. Whatever the sun didn't take, the two-hour walk did.

"Yuh mumma sent me down here to deliver dis ras package fi yuh. Now open up dis rhaatid package so I can see what I mashed up mi body for," commanded Goddie.

Ina untied the sack and unraveled the cloth wrapping. Finally, it was revealed.

Five pieces of fried fish, some yam, some dumplings, and some hair grease.

Goddie hopped up to look closer at the tin. She looked at the open tin and then looked at Ina. She looked back at the tin in disbelief and back at Ina. Her eyes became saucers.

"Yuh madda made me walk almost six miles to deliver fish? Fish!" screamed Goddie.

Ina stood in her confusion.

"My feet are swollen and I'm suffering heat so yuh can have FISH AND HAIR GREASE?"

Goddie began to cry. She looked around at the activity in Annotto Bay. Her eyes caught two young girls her age with beautiful dresses. She watched as the young girls with notebooks weaved their way in the busy crowd while the mothers gossiped, and merchants traded.

She looked back at her hands and feet and then back to the young girls. It was all too much to handle. Her forehead furrowed with confusion as to why a mother would send a child on a six-mile voyage to deliver food to someone living at the port where food is shipped. Goddie could taste the abuse.

Mrs. Sulkett had it in for Goddie from the day she made her ride the truck in the back. Goddie was the help. Her quest to fortify the social order had now come to a head. This was a control exercise. Her attempt to break Goddie was clear.

Ina stood there, confused. She reached out her hand to help Goddie up and was met with a hard swat.

"I've had enough help from your family for one day. Nuh touch me. Don't evah touch me," Goddie snapped as she stood up and brushed the front of her dress off.

Ina looked around. "The bus back to Broadgate should be leaving Annotto Bay in an hour. Yuh can wait for it around the corner, I think. I'm going to give yuh a few shillings to catch it. Wait right here." Ina said, sighing as she disappeared around the corner and inside the building.

"Here yuh go," Ina said as she returned with some money. She came back around the corner to look for Goddie. Flustered, Ina walked around the whole building. It didn't matter.

Goddie was already gone.

# CHAPTER 21

# LAURETTA

———

Goddie opened her eyes slowly. It was the only part of her body that wasn't sore from walking twelve miles in a day. Between the time it took to hike to the north shore and stand up to Ina, Goddie had been walking for over six hours.

Her feet were on fire, and her ankles were swollen grapefruits. She sprained her knee running away from some yard dogs near the river and running to avoid the drunks looking for company. That didn't matter; she would never give Mrs. Sulkett the glory of that information.

Goddie rubbed her knees and suffered in silence. She stretched her arms in the air to examine herself. The callouses on her hands and the dry patches on her arms marked the passage of time. The time for self-care was no longer.

All her waking moments were used as currency to assure the shelter over her head. It all seemed so stupid. Her life was like the Ferris wheel she had read about in school. The morning chatter of the chickens poured water on any remnants of sleep she had left. They were loud this morning. She drew the blanket over her head to shut out the noise and avoid the morning sun. She needed every ounce of reprieve possible. Suddenly, the door to her back room swung open.

"So yuh made it back, eh? Good," barked Mrs. Sulkett.

Goddie said nothing. She didn't have to look to tell the witch was leaning outside Goddie's window. She didn't know anything about that window view until Goddie cleaned it up. As she kept up the wanton chatter, Goddie examined her calloused hands under the blanket as the pathetic taskmaster spewed fake conversation and plastic concern.

"Oh and yes…yuh 'ave quite a bit of work to do before tomorrow. Yuh better get to work if yuh don't want trouble wid me in the mawnin'," barked Mrs. Sulkett. She schlepped herself across the room toward the door and turned back for acknowledgment.

"Yuh had no reason to send me to Annotto Bay yesterday. It's a slave yuh lookin' for. I'm no slave. I see yuh an' so does God. 'member dat," said Goddie from under the blanket.

Mrs. Sulkett walked back toward Goddie's sack bed and leaned into her. "Jus' 'member, ah mi hold the handle and yuh my dear child hold the blade," she whispered.

Goddie's fire rose up and shot right out of the bed, throwing off the blanket and standing toe to toe with the taskmaster. She shoved her calloused finger in the witch's face and leaned forward.

"The grave yuh dig fuh mi, yuh better dig two fi yuh. Judging by the size of yuh backside, yuh might want to dig three," she ran her eyes down Mrs. Sulkett's body.

Goddie wasn't afraid of her anymore. Twelve miles of walking removed all of that. "No wonder yuh nuh 'ave no man nuh more. It's like yuh wake up and eat misery for breakfast, nasty for lunch, and bitter for dinner. Yuh name really suits yuh. Yuh love to sulk."

Mrs. Sulkett raised her hand to box Goddie.

Goddie raised her chin but never broke her stare. "When yuh box mi yuh bettah kill mi the first time or run," she whispered. The awkward silence calmed the oppressor's hand.

"Just 'member, yuh a di one going to be homeless if yuh don't finish whut I tell you to finish," she said as she stormed out the back room, slamming the door. The loud bang sent the chickens outside the window into confusion as they fluttered around talking among themselves.

Goddie sat back on her sack bed.

*Daadie. Are you out there? Do you still see me? Do you see this? I am far from our lighthouse now. I'm in this sea of despair, and my boat is sinking. Do you still see me, Daadie? She has taken my light and my strength. My hands show the wear, but my heart wears the despair.*

*Do you see me, Daadie? Do you still see me?*

She pulled her father's Bible out of the pillowcase and rested it on her lap. The grass blades that marked his passages still held their position. Goddie picked the oldest-looking grass blade and cracked open the thick book. Her eyes lit up as her Daadie spoke to her.

*The LORD is my light and my salvation; whom shall I fear? The LORD is the strength of my life; of whom shall I be afraid?*
*When the wicked, even mine enemies and my foes, came upon me to eat up my flesh, they stumbled and fell.*

*Well, this one sure is wicked*, thought Goddie. She walked the Bible over to the windowsill and kept reading.

> *One thing have I desired of the LORD, that will I seek after; that I may dwell in the house of the LORD all the days of my life, to behold the beauty of the LORD, and to inquire in his temple.*
> *For in the time of trouble he shall hide me in his pavilion: in the secret of his tabernacle shall he hide me; he shall set me up upon a rock. (King James Bible, Psalm 27:1-2, 4-5)*

"Psalm 27," Goddie whispered to herself.

She took out the withering grass blade and replaced it with a torn piece of ribbon on the floor. She gently closed the book and cast her eyes at the pile of clothes waiting for repair.

"Goddie, I'm heading to town for a while. Mek sure yuh start with the long dress. I need that bright and early tomorrow mawnin'," Mrs. Sulkett barked.

She forgot she had just threatened Goddie a few minutes ago. Goddie didn't answer. She listened as the taskmaster drove away in the old rusty truck.

*Who knew the devil could drive?* Goddie thought.

She pulled the long dress off the pile and made quick work of the hem repair Mrs. Sulkett requested. As much as she hated her, she needed her for now until a better way came forth.

She got up, brushed the front of her housedress, and threw the finished dress over her shoulder.

"I'll drop this in her room and fix some tea," she muttered to herself as she made her way to Mrs. Sulkett's room.

Goddie dropped the dress off on her bed and turned to walk out. She almost made it through the threshold when her eyes caught something strange. Near the doorframe was a small antique shelf with various items on it. On the bottom shelf was a strange wooden box with a lid on a brass hinge. The box was open, and she could see a group of letters.

Goddie always knew the letter envelopes from the red and white markings Daadie used to show her. This was different though. She leaned in closer to read the top letter.

"O-r-m-s..," she spelled out. A napkin partially covered the front of the envelope, so she reached in and pulled out the stack of letters all bound in a bow. She stopped breathing.

Goddie rummaged through eight months worth of letters from her siblings.

For months, Goddie had asked if there had been any communication from Spring Hill and the answer was always no. She thought her brothers and sisters had banished her. For months, she grieved the loss of her parents and her siblings.

Her heart sank at the injustice. She quickly caught her breath and gathered herself. She saw some blank envelopes on the top shelf, stuffed them in the box, and replaced the napkin. She gently closed the box, straightened the items on the shelf, and left the room door ajar as she had found it.

Goddie dove into her bed and laid out all the letters. She put them in order by date and opened the first one. Most of them were from Lauretta except for the last one. It was from Lambert.

The letters were thick with pages, including all kinds of notes from the other siblings, drawings from Lassie, and complete with grease marks on the corners. Lauretta updated her on the younger siblings, the happenings of Spring Hill, and the recent relatives that passed away.

She continued reading and learned how the farm was doing. Goddie even got word that her friend Ann was asking about her. Ann's family sent her away to live in England with her aunt to complete her education. Goddie feasted on the updates.

She finally opened the last letter in the stack from Lambert.

*"Dear Goddie,*

*I am sorry to write this news, as it is my wish to tell you in person. Lauretta and some friends were at the Colongolook River. They caught some Janga shrimp and cooked it up for dinner. We don't know what happened, but she fell very ill.*

*All the villagers tried to doctor her up, but she was vomiting so much and running a high fever. It looked like she developed worms in her belly. We tried everything.*

*Lauretta died two days ago. We think the Janga poisoned her, but we aren't sure. We don't think we can keep her long. The elders say we have to bury her within the week because of the heat. We will wait for you as long as possible. Try and come home.*

Goddie's tears blotted the last sentence from Lambert. She read the letter again and again and again, digesting every consonant like food. She looked at the date of the letter. She looked at the calendar on the wall.

Lauretta died three months ago.

Mrs. Sulkett had done the abominable. She knew that if her family wanted Goddie to come home, she would lose her free labor temporarily or maybe forever.

"LAURETTA!" Goddie cried as she clutched the letters. She screamed her name in anguish as the chickens rustled to the disturbance.

"LAURETT…"

"Lau…"

Goddie gasped for air as her breaking heart tried to keep pace with her lungs. She heaved in sorrow as she read the letters again and again. She sat on her sack bed and stared into the wall. Her thoughts became blank, exhausted from all the yelling. She slumped against the wall. In mercy, her body gave out and she fell asleep on top of her letters.

It was all too much.

The squealing brakes of Mrs. Sulkett's truck signaled her return from town. She had been gone all day. Goddie opened her eyes and regained her bearings. She had to be smart now. She had to turn her anger into angles. Loathing must transfer into logic. Mrs. Sulkett had the handle, but Goddie held the blade, and blades can be bent.

She quickly wiped her tears, gathered her letters, and stuffed them into the pillowcase with Daadie's Bible. She stood up, brushed the front of her housedress, and quickly started to let out the hem in one of the dresses in the pile.

Without knocking, Mrs. Sulkett swung her door open.

"Yuh 'ave the long dress mi ask you to fix?" barked the woman.

"Yes, Mrs. Sulkett. I put it on yuh bed so yuh could see it first thing," answered Goddie. She trained her eyes on her master. All Goddie's movements from now on had to be choreographed. She had leverage she had never had before and wasting it in anger would be a mistake. All thoughts had to be processed in rigor before she allowed her mouth to release them.

"Ma'am, mi stomach nuh feel too good. I think my monthly is heavy this time. We nuh have enough products. Is it possible to get some tomorrow? I really need it," Goddie said as she rubbed her stomach.

"Yuh 'ave pain?"

"Yes, ma'am. Lots of pain. Could use some pain powder as well," Goddie explained.

"Alright, I'll have to go to Port Antonio tomorrow to get that medicine. Annotto Bay won't 'ave it. I'll leave early morning and should be back after lunch. Rest yuhself."

Mrs. Sulkett felt Goddie's forehead and looked at her again. Goddie winced in pain and doubled over on the bed.

"Alright, guh sleep."

"Yes, ma'am," Goddie replied. The taskmaster closed her door gently and went into her bedroom. Feeling her forehead had been the only act of kindness she had shown Goddie in over a year. It didn't matter now.

Goddie was leaving tomorrow.

# PART V

# WINDRUSH BABY

# CHAPTER 22

# THREE CHICKENS

---

The morning breeze blew strong through the back room of the house, flushing out Mrs. Sulkett's spirit from the evening prior.

Goddie kept her eyes closed tight until the sound of the rusty old truck faded into the morning. Vera and Ruth went to Port Antonio with their mother for the company, and Ms. Maude didn't join the living until mid-morning.

It was time.

Goddie flung her blanket to the corner of the room and got to work.

Her plan wasn't perfect, but it was hers. Escape the house. Catch the bus to Kingston. Don't get caught. Simple.

She couldn't go back to Spring Hill. Mrs. Sulkett and her daughters would come looking for her there, and besides, Lauretta was already in the ground. Spring Hill had no jobs. No friends. No alternatives. She had a whole day to decide where she would lay her head, but she knew she couldn't spend another night in this demon's house.

The floor in the house gave away all the secrets, and every footstep was measured by the planks. She methodically gathered her clothes and stuffed them into a potato sack. She tied the letters together and quietly grabbed her green dress off the hook on the wall.

A ragged scarf was tied around her head to control her locks. She had already sweated out her housedress.

Goddie made her bed and tidied up the back room to perfection. A few extra pieces of clothes from the repair pile were stuffed into the bag. She took a second bag and headed straight to Mrs. Sulkett's room. She was a witch, but she had the best hair products and irons. It was time for a little self-reparation.

"Yuh ah come with me," she whispered as she dumped some of the curling kits and irons into the sack.

The glory of escape and redemption would have to wait. She took every precaution just in case Ms. Maude woke up early. The last thing she needed was Ms. Maude asking questions that would slow her down.

"There we go. All packed," she whispered.

Goddie lowered her bags out of the window near the chicken coop. She had planned to take the path behind the house to connect to the main road. Her heart kept triple time in her throat with every maneuver. Sweat ran down her face as she evaluated every move.

She could hear Ms. Maude moving around in her bedroom. Goddie figured this would be the morning that swaaty woman would wake up early.

It was time to go. The plan was to catch the midday bus to Kingston and find shelter somewhere.

She grabbed her last dress off Vera's hook and threw it over her head. She brushed off the front of the dress and looked up in the mirror.

"It looks better on me anyway. Time to go." Goddie smiled and walked out the front door and around to the side of the house.

Goddie looked around before picking up her sacks and heading down the path to the main road. She decided her best bet was to catch the bus at Mr. Chin's store. It would take a few hours to reach the Half Way Tree bus terminal in Kingston, and she could figure it out from there.

She stopped in her tracks. There was one problem though. The bus to Kingston would cost at least a pound. With the few pounds she needed for food, she didn't have the fare. Sweat ran down her face as she searched for answers. She was leaving, even if she had to walk to Kingston.

Goddie returned to the side of the house and crouched down, crippled with fear. As much as she wanted to, she couldn't walk to Kingston with the sacks, and Mrs. Sulkett would be back any moment.

Her presence in front of the chicken coop rustled the brood, and the noise picked up.

"Shhh, shhh." She threw a rock at the coop, scolding the chickens. The rock activated the remaining flock, and now she had a problem. The neighbor's head poked out the back door to see what the commotion was.

Then it all became clear. Goddie smiled to herself and rose in her confidence.

"Yuh coming with me."

Goddie grabbed three chickens by the neck and stuffed them in her sack. Their feathers flew everywhere, but that didn't matter. She remembered how Mr. Chin made a satchel out of a potato sack, and she made quick work with the machete against the tree.

It was time.

A half-smile came to her face as the last phase of escape was revealed. She flung open all the doors to the chicken coop. Mrs. Sulkett's prized hens went running for the road at the first sight of freedom.

With the pride of a thousand queens, Goddie held her head up and quietly walked around the back of the house and down a small path to the main road. All she had to do was make it to the store. She looked behind one last time, exhaled, and started running.

Goddie ran for her life. She became a gazelle as her legs consumed the road with each stride. The chickens squawked in fear as they swung from side to side. The morning breeze kept the heat at bay as the gazelle in the headscarf carved up the road with speed.

With great expediency, she reached the tiny road shop quickly and stumbled to the back of the building for fear of being seen by Mrs. Sulkett. Her truck would be passing any second now. She dropped her bags and knocked on the back door. She brushed off the front of her dress and straightened up.

"Ah, it's my walker friend. How are you?" asked Mr. Chin.

He looked at his sweaty guest and the bags behind her. His smile went straight as he returned his gaze to his young visitor.

"Leaving?"

"I've got to get away from her," Goddie explained between gasps. "I've just got to get away. I need your help."

Mr. Chin leaned against the backdoor frame, waiting for the proposition from the sweaty girl.

"I don't have enough for all the bus fare to Kingston. She never paid me, so I don't have much money. I'm not begging yuh money, but......," explained Goddie.

"But what?" questioned Mr. Chin.

Goddie stepped back off the step toward her bags. She grabbed the bag with the live chickens and opened the top, revealing her captives. The chickens were restless, but they were prime birds with full feather growth and strong bodies. They fluttered around in the bag at the promise of freedom, releasing a cloud of feathers into the air.

Goddie held the bag up. "If you'll buy these from me, I'll have enough for the bus and some food."

"How much do you want fuh dem?" questioned the shopkeeper.

"Whatever will get me to Kingston and buy a meal."

The shopkeeper looked in the bag again. He felt the body of one of the birds and then closed it up. He cast his gaze on the young girl and saw himself. Not long ago, he was on a boat arriving in Port Antonio to work the fields. He knew what it meant to be scared.

"Wait here," he said.

Goddie leaned against the back wall of the shop. She gathered her bags together and closed her eyes tight.

*God, if yuh sent your son to die for me, see me 'ere and now. Deliver me.*

"Here yuh go. Bettah hurry up. Yuh bus soon come," Mr. Chin said.

Goddie opened her eyes slowly. She would take whatever would get her on the bus. She knew she needed at least a pound to make it to Kingston. She could figure out the food when she got to the city. She held out her hand and kept her eyes to the ground. She felt the banknotes and the coins hit her palms, but she wasn't sure if it would be enough. If he gave her a few pence, she would have to walk to Kingston. She wasn't going back.

"Look up nuh?" Mr. Chin asked as he closed her hands.

Goddie unwrapped her fingers to reveal five pounds in her sweaty palms. She looked at him as the tears ran.

"I hear the bus. Yuh bett....."

Goddie jumped into his arms and squeezed him. She left her tears on his shirt as she gathered her sacks and ran around to the front of the store.

The roar of the bus came around the corner. The black smoke out the back announced its presence. As she got into position, she saw something she had prayed not to see.

Goddie knew the front of Mrs. Sulkett's rusty truck anywhere. The road wasn't wide enough to pass, so the truck was relegated to trailing the bus through town. She pulled her headscarf under her eyebrows and kept her head down.

The bus squealed to a stop. She turned her head to the right to see Vera looking straight at her. Goddie held her breath and climbed onto the bus. She shimmied herself to the back and piled her bags near her. The bus loaded the remaining passengers and after an eternity, finally closed the door. Goddie kept her head down, but her eyes trained on the window.

Mercifully, the bus eased off the brake and pulled off. She raised her head in enough time to see Mr. Chin's face. He wiped a tear in his eye as he waved goodbye.

"Thank you," she whispered and blew him a kiss through the open window.

The bus traveled about a mile down the road before the opportunity to pass came. Goddie saw the small truck pass the bus on her side of the window. As she looked out, her eyes locked in on Vera as they passed each other.

Vera's eyes locked in on her. Goddie pulled her sack up to cover half her face. Vera stared at the stranger with the headscarf, but her face never registered it was Goddie.

The truck sped past the bus and went ahead down the road.

For the first time in hours, Goddie exhaled and wiped her face. She put her sacks beside her and rested her arm on the windowsill.

She brushed the front of her dress, removed her headscarf, and let the midday breeze hit her in the face.

*Thank you, God. Thank you, Daadie.*

Goddie was free.

## CHAPTER 23

# SHOPKEEPER'S SALVATION

———

It took Goddie two years to grow into city life. At almost twenty years old, she had experienced more than most adults twice her age. The city of Kingston was a beehive of activity compared to Blue Mountain. The trees of Portland parish gave way to the hum of cars and trucks racing here and there in the city of merchants and traders.

The allure of spice imports and sugar exports made Kingston a key junction of commerce and transportation. The ports welcomed people of all kinds. Jamaica's population now included Chinese, Indians, and some Europeans.

Goddie thought Kingston was vibrant but soon learned it was also dangerous. The gap between the haves and the have-nots was cavernous. The disparity in the socioeconomic fabric meant crime was prevalent in the city of three hundred thousand.

She quickly learned that the story of Jamaicans was a complex one. The remnants of the slave trade laid scars on the land, but its story was always about its people. From the gutter-most to the uttermost, Kingston showed the stratification of change.

Goddie contemplated as she sat and looked out into Half Way Tree junction. Her first two years in Kingston had given her an education in who really held the handle and who really held the blade.

She learned that the Chinese, Indians, and Europeans were given the highest access to capital, whereby they could develop the infrastructure to secure more commerce and eventually wealth. Jamaican natives were largely relegated to small and medium-sized businesses. Despite being the capital of the Spaniards long ago, the native Jamaicans always remained the group on the outside looking in. They didn't teach this part in Spring Hill.

"Yuh sleepin' or whuh?" the commanding voice said from the back of the store.

Goddie wiped the daydream from her eyes and stood up straight. "No, Mr. Hammil, I'm just looking at di people dem and watching' di traffic."

"I need yuh to watch di traffic while movin' dis broom from side to side."

Mr. Hammil grabbed the broom handle off the wall and shoved it in her face. Goddie smiled as she slid off the stool and took the handle of the broom. She knew the evening crowd would be rushing in soon, and the store needed to be swept. Nobody likes to buy food from a dirty place.

Goddie knew better than to cross Mr. Hammil. He had given her a home when she was homeless and work when she was starving. Kingston was going through a revitalization, and it was not uncommon to find small shops sandwiched between larger new buildings. Commercial development was strong, but property rights were stronger and small shop owners didn't bow easily to commercial raids on their livelihood.

*** 

Two years before, Goddie had walked for hours from district to district until her eye caught the sign "Help Wanted" through the bars of the white gate. Behind the bars slept two Doberman pinschers who looked like they ate unemployed females for dinner. After she knocked on the gate with a rock, a dark, lean man slowly approached.

His name was Pharez Alphonso Hammil. He knew the area where Daadie and Mumma were from and decided to take a chance on her. She was sweaty, grimy, and tired, but he saw past that. He knew a worker when he saw one. Mr. Hammil let her take a room in the back of the store in exchange for lower pay. It was perfect. He was moving slower, and the help was sorely needed. She wanted to honor Daadie by doing whatever Mr. Hammil asked. She knew her good fortune was all Daadie's doing.

Mr. Hammil poked his head around the corner again. "When yuh finish, I want to talk to you. Come outside to the front of the store."

"Yes, sir," she replied.

Goddie swept the entire store and put the dogs in the back. After she wiped down the counters and straightened the cans, she headed outside.

"Did you need something, Mr. Hammil?"

Mr. Hammil pointed to a seat next to him. "Come and sit down."

"When yuh banged on my gate a few years ago, I didn't think much of yuh outside of a store clerk." He rubbed his dry, rusty hands together as they both sat on the bench watching rush hour traffic.

"Yuh have grown into a wonderful young lady. Whatever it is that brought yuh here, yuh have faced it and grown past it. I see how yuh work so hard fuh me, and yuh never let me down. I can only wonder to myself that there must be more yuh want to do."

"I want to go to school and learn something. Maybe sewing or something," Goddie expressed. She took his cue to stretch her long legs out in front of the bench as she listened. She had been standing most of the day, and her feet had swollen.

Mr. Hammil rubbed his head top and turned to look at Goddie. "Yuh parents trained yuh well. I can see by the way yuh handle the customers dem and care the store yuh should be putting more knowledge in yuh brains."

Goddie raised her head as he continued.

"I'm glad to have yuh, but I want you to know I don't want to hold yuh. If it's school yuh want, don't be afraid to fly. Go after what it is yuh want. Life doesn't come fuh yuh. You have to go and tek it."

As Goddie looked at Mr. Hammil, he squeezed her hand and her eyes got misty. He was the closest thing to Daadie she had felt in a long time.

Mr. Hammil leaned back against the store and continued, "Don't mek yuh life pass yuh. When you see the chance, be ready to jump. It doesn't matter who yuh leave behind. To start is to live. Remember, yuh didn't come to Kingston to count cows. Yuh came to drink milk."

They both laughed as Goddie remembered that old proverb from Daadie. Daadie used to beat that into the boys when they were in the field. Mr. Hammil was right, and she loved him all the more for acknowledging it.

"In the meantime, get inside an' serve these people," he suggested as he got up and walked around the building.

Goddie spread a smile on her face, hopped up, and ran behind the counter to help the hungry rush-hour crowd.

After the crowd thinned out, she went to the back to check store inventory. She grabbed an old wooden crate and straddled her long body over the box so she could get an accurate count. Her mind focused on cans and crops as she went through the shelves in detail.

"Four more mackerel, seven bully beef, three pounds ah flour, and ten bag ah rice." she whispered.

"Hello, anybody in di back?" Cried an odd-sounding voice. Goddie had heard the voice before but couldn't place its origin. She stood up from the crate to listen to it again.

"Hi dere. Anyone in di back?"

"Yes, ma'am, one moment. I'm on my way," Goddie replied as she gathered her inventory papers and moved the crate to the side. The second reply heightened her intrigue as she motioned toward the front of the store.

She brushed off the front of her shop apron and straightened her hair clip. She turned the corner and saw the owner of the voice standing with her back to her, looking out at the busyness of Kingston.

Goddie walked past the counter and approached the stranger to get a good look. The stranger had some luggage and a hat, so Goddie still wasn't sure who it was. At first, she worried it could be Mrs. Sulkett, but she sounded too young and too happy to be that taskmaster.

Goddie's heart clogged her throat as she walked up to the strange female.

"Yes, ma'am, how can I help you?" Goddie positioned herself as she steadied herself for the reveal.

She caught a look at the lady's hands before she saw her face, and she knew Mrs. Sulkett's miserable self never had such pretty hands. The stranger turned from the window and ...

"Goddie?"

"Sandra?......SANDRA?" screamed Goddie.

"GODDDIEEE!" screamed the stranger.

"It's me. It's me, Sandra." The stranger dropped her belongings on the shop floor and grabbed Goddie for dear life. The young ladies held each other and jumped up and down as they erupted in joy.

Mr. Hammil poked his head around the corner to see the commotion, but he didn't say anything.

Sandra was the oldest sister of Ann, Goddie's neighbor and childhood friend from Spring Hill. The last time Goddie saw Ann, it was the day Mumma died.

Goddie grew up knowing both siblings, but she was best friends with Ann as they were the same age and school level. Goddie stood back and stared at Sandra. She looked like new money. She wasn't tall, but she filled out in all the right places and her eyes were bright with stories of a new adventure.

Goddie took in her smile as Sandra lit up the room. Her aura said that she had been places and seen things. Sandra had always looked like Ann. The sisters shared the same facial construction and body type. Sandra smiled like Ann and even hugged like Ann. Goddie wiped away a runaway tear.

"How is your sister?" inquired Goddie as she admired the Harrod's tag on Sandra's dress.

"Ann is well, mi dear. Mother sent her off to live in London. She lives with our auntie and uncle. They had been trying to convince her for years. She wasn't always willing to go. The decision got easier after...well, yuh know."

"Yeah, I know," Goddie replied.

"She cried for you for days, Goddie. Even in London, she grieved you for over a year. You two were together your whole lives, and one day yuh just disappeared. You left her alone without a friend, and she hurt a long time over that. It was like yuh died, and there was no funeral," explained Sandra as she wiped Goddie's tears.

Goddie heaved in sorrow at the realization of the damage. She grabbed Sandra and held her tight.

"I didn't have any say, Sandra. I didn't have any say," she repeated as her heart heaved everything she had held for three years. Goddie pushed back from Sandra and looked her in the eyes. "Please tell Ann I had no say. I'm so, so sorry," she pleaded as she held her head down and wept.

After a moment, she looked up. "Is Ann happy?"

"She is. She'll be even happier when she hears I spoke to you. She always talked about how smart you were and how you were cheated because your parents died at the same time."

Goddie nodded as she returned her gaze to the ground. Even Sandra's toes looked like they had a good life.

"Yuh stay here?" asked Sandra.

"Yes, I stay here and mind the shop. I live in the back."

"Ok excellent. God is good. I came into the shop because I wasn't sure where the Half Way Tree bus junction was. I'm headed to the country tonight. I'm only here for a few weeks to see everybody and bring medicine for mother. Her arthritis is acting rough now," explained Sandra.

"It's around the corner down by the clock tower," instructed Goddie.

After an awkward pause, Goddie looked back at Mr. Hammil. He nodded at the anticipation of the question.

"Gwaan, mon. Walk her to the bus terminal. Hurry back. The sun is setting."

Goddie jumped up as she untied her shop apron, brushed the front of her dress, and grabbed one of Sandra's bags. The young ladies gushed at the chance to spend a few more moments together.

Mr. Hammil pushed a piece of bun and some cheese in Sandra's travel bag and took Goddie's apron from her. The young ladies walked out the door, past the white gate, and into the vibrancy of Kingston. Mr. Hammil smiled as he watched happiness walk around the corner.

Throughout the coming weeks, Goddie tried hard not to think about Sandra, Ann, or memories of Spring Hill. Seeing Sandra opened up old memories of Daadie and Mumma. She decided to quiet her mind by helping Mr. Hammil.

It had been four months since Sandra's visit. By then, the exhilaration of seeing Sandra had long worn off, and any ideations of what-if had long passed their expiration date. Goddie settled back into life on Hope Road. The gumbo of speeding taxis, grinding buses, and makeshift merchant carts created a kaleidoscope of Kingston.

The city was alive with murmurs of Jamaican independence from the United Kingdom. Day after day, Mr. Hammil kept tabs on the independence news and word from relatives about what London was thinking. Every week, Goddie would sort out the mail for Mr. Hammil. His correspondence with relatives from Toronto, New York, and London made for a steady stream of global insight.

Things would change five months later when Sunny the postman tapped the gate to the store. He would have come in except the dogs were roaming.

Goddie waved from inside the store. "Hi, Sunny. I'm coming." She came out and exchanged a glass of sorrel for the pile of mail he had tied with a string. It wasn't unusual to get a lot of mail in one day.

"Yuh might want to pay attention to the pile," Sunny explained as he sipped the cool drink. "The top envelope ah fi yuh."

"Me?"

"Yes, ma'am," Sunny replied as he handed back the empty glass.

"Ok. Thanks, Sunny."

The sun was bright, so Goddie stepped under the tree. She wanted to enjoy the afternoon breeze while she went through the mail.

The envelope was thick with red and blue international markings on the front. Even the dogs came, wandering around to see what was going on. They lay down beside her to get the gossip. She stopped breathing as she read the front.

*Fr: Ann Francis*
*1990 Duntroon Cres. Apt 31*
*London, UK SE24 0BB*

"She didn't forget me," Goddie whispered. She gently broke the seal and slid her thumb under the flap. She slowly opened the letter. Her body drifted down the trunk of the tree as she brought her knees closer.

With each breath, she unfolded the pages as gently as possible. Ann's handwriting was all she needed to see. Goddie held the letter to her chest and exhaled.

*Thank you, Daadie. You still see me.*

Goddie knew she wasn't forgotten.

# CHAPTER 24

# ANN'S LETTER

———

Every morning for the last three weeks, Goddie pulled out the letter from Ann. She read every line like it was the first time and consumed every syllable like it was nourishment for the day.

On this particular morning, she pulled her pillow over her head and laughed herself into hysteria. It was like a sweet song on a Sabbath morning.

*Dear Goddie,*

*The best joy ever was the news that you were alive and well. My heart was full knowing you were doing ok in Kingston. Sandra wrote me and gave me all the details.*

*The day I heard you left in the back of that truck was the saddest day of my life. My heart broke when my mother said you were taken away in the rain by yourself. It was all very confusing for me. Where did they send you? Why did they send you away? What did you do? I cried for a long time. I miss my friend so very much and I long to see you again. I spoke with my aunt and uncle about you, and I wanted to offer you something.*

*The United Kingdom has opened up to allow some Jamaicans to come for sponsored education. My auntie works at St. Andrews Hospital in Northampton, UK. The hospital is about one hour north of London and is looking to sponsor training for psyche nursing students. The only requirement is that immigrants to the United Kingdom come from within the commonwealth and must be sponsored by a letter from a resident. I explained your situation to my aunt, and she has agreed to sponsor you. God we praise. I will be sending an official sponsor letter that you will need to enter the country.*

*Goddie, please write me and send your official legal name so we can complete the sponsor letter. I am going to enter the nursing program, and I think you would make a good nurse as well. God is good. My auntie said she can sponsor the letter, but you would need to pay the fare to London.*

*It is very important you do not tell anyone. Too many bad mind people. Keep this secret in your chest. Send your information to me as soon as possible. This may take several months, so we must move quickly. Save your money and write me when you think you'll be able to save all the fare. I praise God that auntie is willing to help you have a new start. It was my only wish for you.*

*Please write me. Remember, do not tell anyone. You don't want to ruin your chance.*

*All my love,*
*Ann.*

When she first received the letter, Goddie tried to contain herself. She couldn't afford the heartbreak of being let down.

She dutifully sent off her information to Ann and expected nothing in return. She didn't think about it. It was just easier that way. Several weeks later, Goddie watched Sunny walk up to the gate.

"Another envelope fuh yuh, Goddie," Sunny said as he passed the precious envelope with red and blue markings to her through the gate.

"It's probably holiday greetings from my friend," Goddie replied as she tucked the envelope under her arm and strolled back to the shop.

Mr. Hammil looked up from his afternoon paper. "Another letter from Sandra?"

"I think so." Goddie giggled as she scurried toward her room in the back of the shop.

Mr. Hammil watched his shopkeeper act very strangely. Just the presence of the letter lit up Goddie's face and changed the mood of the shop. It was nice to see her so happy. He pressed a smile across his face and returned to his newspaper.

The new envelope from Ann was thicker than any she had received before. She studied the outside and noticed strange markings on the envelope.

*Fr: Barrington Barristers and Solicitors*
*On behalf of George and Bernette Francis*
*45 Lincoln's Inn's Field, London, UK*
*WC2A 3LJ*

Goddie sat in the middle of her bedroom floor and stared at the paper.

This was it. She was leaving Jamaica. She pulled the pillowcase from under her bed and removed her Daadie's Bible. She wrapped the letter in an old cloth and shoved it in the pillowcase.

"Everything ok, Goddie? We have customers out front," Mr. Hammil complained. "Where are yuh?"

"I'm coming now," Goddie said as she shoved the pillowcase back under the bed. She stood up, brushed the front of her shop apron off, and slowly walked toward the back room door.

She turned back and stared at the bed.

*Keep this safe for me, Daadie. Love you.*

With that, she put her face straight and went out front to serve customers.

# CHAPTER 25

# A DAUGHTER'S GOODBYE

———

Goddie dragged the bottle torch closer to her side. The kerosene sloshed around at precarious levels, and the flame whipped any which way without responsibility.

Daadie had always warned her to be careful. Its flame was an unfaithful friend and could not be trusted. She had to be vigilant not to attract attention. Mr. Hammil's snoring rattled the metal bed frame upstairs, but she took no precautions.

Today was the day. She tucked herself into the corner of the back room and committed to memory the words Daadie taught her in times of trouble.

*He that dwelleth in the secret place of the Most High shall abide under the shadow of the Almighty.*
*I will say of the LORD, He is my refuge and my fortress: my God; in him will I trust.*
*Surely he shall deliver thee from the snare of the fowler, and from the noisome pestilence. (King James Bible, Psalms 91:1-3)*

She tucked her knees up close and leaned into her Daadie's Bible. The voyage ahead would take all the girding she could convoke. She had waited six months for this moment.

She moved in silence as she arranged all the documents and permissions needed to travel overseas. She kept her word to Ann and uttered nothing. The only person who knew she was leaving Jamaica was the lady who sold her the ticket. The betrayal of her siblings and Mr. Hammil would be a cross she would bear eternally.

She couldn't worry about that today though. She stared off into the night as the peeny wallie bugs played in the nautical blackness. The night had kept watch as she steadied her mind. Daydreams of deferred dreams became night dreams of what it seems were the eminence of a renaissance. Her rebirth was near. A smile crossed her face as she turned the page in Daadie's Bible.

*Because he hath set his love upon me, therefore will I deliver him: I will set him on high, because he hath known my name.*
*He shall call upon me, and I will answer him: I will be with him in trouble; I will deliver him, and honor him. With long life will I satisfy him, and shew him my salvation. (King James Bible, Psalm 91:14-16)*

The roaming dogs outside sniffed around her open window. Goddie put her father's Bible to the side and stood up to lean on the windowsill. Her ears recorded the sounds of the spring rain pouring off the house.

The rain had become a sign. It rained when Daadie died, when they buried Mumma, and when they sent her away. It always rained. No matter its significance this time, this rain only meant she would need to cover her head. Goddie was getting on that boat even if the whole earth opened up and swallowed Kingston.

She reached under the bed and pulled a small suitcase she had plundered from the back shed. It looked a thousand years old, but the latches worked, and it wasn't heavy. After a few minutes with a wet rag, she decided it was worthy of a trip to the United Kingdom.

Once again, she gathered all her clothes together and stuffed them into the suitcase. She tied her letters together and grabbed that old green dress off the hook on the wall. At last, with her entire life, a mere collection of some old clothes, a few letters, and her Daadie's Bible, Goddie quietly closed the latches on the small suitcase. She grabbed two tins of bully beef and some hardo bread from the store inventory and stuffed them into a sack.

The rain persisted like an insufferable toddler. She bundled up and double wrapped her head with a long headscarf. Goddie only had one problem. The front entrance gate to the house was padlocked, and Mr. Hammil had the only key on his key ring. There was only one way out, and she needed to act quickly.

She found some old twine and tied it around the handle of the suitcase. She cut a few more lengths and tied them around the sack handles. The window was on the main floor, so it was just high enough for her to lower herself down without falling.

"Birth certificate, boarding pass, destination address, and two hundred pounds," she whispered as she audited her papers. She wrapped them up again and placed them deep in the sack with Daadie's' Bible. As she withdrew her hand from the sack, she grabbed a note she had written earlier.

*Dear Mr. Hammil,*

*When my father died, I didn't think I would get a chance to have another father. You opened the door to a young girl from the country. You didn't have to. You trusted me with your business and your reputation.*

*I'm sorry I had to leave like this. I couldn't bear to say goodbye to two fathers in one lifetime.*

*Thank you,*
*Goddie.*

She stuffed two pieces of leftover chicken into her dress pocket and stepped through the window. As her two feet hit the mud outside, the Doberman pinschers marched around the corner. With a quick flick of the wrist, she threw the chicken pieces to the deepest part of the kennel and shut the gate behind them.

She wasn't even outside five minutes, and she was completely soaked from the rain. Today, that didn't matter. "I've got twenty-one days to dry off," she assured herself and grabbed her luggage.

The boarding time for the Sandell Brothers Irpinia ship was two hours away, so she had to hurry. The main gate to Hope Road. was left unlocked, so she slipped herself through the bars and pressed into the torrent. Goddie hugged the buildings close as she jumped from curb to curb.

Her shoes and socks, stained with rainwater, sloshed around as Goddie picked up her pace in the storm. She ran down Old Hope Road for a few blocks but stopped to rest near Nuttall Hospital for a few minutes. She didn't want to spend what little money she had on expensive taxis, but forty minutes of rain abuse was enough for her. Kingston had plenty of taxis, but one had to be wary of taxis roaming around before dawn. She looked up to see dawn was about to break, so she kept on walking. She would rather be wet than missing.

Maxfield Avenue came up quickly as she tightened up her coat and trudged through the rain. She remembered that Maxfield Avene went straight past Trench Town and on to the port. It wouldn't be long now. Goddie walked fast, keeping her eyes on the curb and the next building. Passing the homeless and stray dogs was a potent reminder. Stopping wasn't an option.

*Well, Daadie, see me out here? I'm leaving the safety of a warm bed to go and see what God and the world have in store for me. I'm not going to act brave right now, Daadie, because I'm scared. Real scared. Who leaves their house to walk two miles in the rain to catch a boat? My dress is wet, but my heart is dry and ready. Change in life is never perfect, but I've learned that's what makes it perfect. I know you and Mumma are watching me. Thank you.*

With mercy, the rain ceased and the darkness broke to reveal the promise of the day. The final trek to the port through Greenwich Town and past Maypen Cemetery went fast, as Goddie was soon surrounded by the busyness of Kingston. The street vendors started the day's gossip, and merchants rolled their goods into position. Goddie looked around in wonder. It would be a long time before she heard the sounds of Jamaica again.

"Ahh, Jamaica, yuh stay good yuh 'ear?" she whispered. "Mi love yuh always. But it's time to see more and start over."

She pressed on down Marcus Garvey Drive toward the boarding office. The closer she walked to the port, the thicker the crowd became. Passengers from all walks of Jamaica were making their way to the steel fortress floating in the sea. The final corner came. The sign said Kingston Freeport Terminal, but it may as well have said The Port of No Return.

The joy of something new quickly converted into the heaviness of the long goodbye. Even the bravest of souls had to leave what was familiar and cleave to their new mother. A five-hundred-foot steel hull held together with rivets and welding. A mother with an unforgiving bosom on which its passengers must lay.

Goddie imagined how the grand Irpina ship had seen this scene many times before. It wouldn't be the first time it opened her bosom to receive its load. It floated patiently as strangers on the shore became siblings onboard. A strange brew of individuals bound by a common thread; they were all leaving Jamaica indefinitely.

To Irpina, strangers that became family onboard would soon simply be cargo—items to be counted, fed, and stored until delivered to Southampton, UK. The simmering reality started to boil, and lines formed, and goodbyes began. Goddie watched as parents gripped their children in grief and wives wiped the tears of their husbands. One by one, the goodbyes concluded, and travelers advanced toward the gangplank.

Soon it would be Goddie's turn.

A loud, guttural East Hackney accent broke the moment without apology. "Papers, ma'am."

Goddie turned around and stared at the miserable dump of a man. The hardened creases in his face told the story of a life at sea for far too long.

"Pardon, sir?" she asked.

"I said PAPERS, MA'AM. Gaze when you get on the boat. Let's GO!" said the officer.

"Yes, sir," she responded.

Goddie reached into the sack holding Daadie's Bible and pulled out the paperwork she had protected for months. The officer snatched it out of her hands and reviewed the details.

"V-E-T-A. Umm, ma'am, how do you pronounce this name?"

"It's pronounced "VEE-TAH.""

The moments seemed like forever as he reviewed her birth certificate, boarding pass, and final destination paperwork. "Alright then. Heading to Southampton, UK, are you?" he questioned as he organized his stamps.

"Yes, sir, I am."

He banged the official stamps on her boarding pass with all the aggression of a man longing for a friend. "Welcome aboard, Veta Ormsby. Watch your step on the gangplank."

Before that day, Goddie had only used her identification to register for school. She had almost forgotten that Veta was her legal name and that no one outside of Jamaica would care less about a person named Goddie. Nicknames didn't matter in the big world. A world sequenced by legality and formality wants only the official version, not Daadie's version.

Legal not pseudo would be the agenda of the day. Daadie gave her that name, but for now, even he would agree the nickname would have to rest in her heart. The last vestige of Spring Hill had been taken away. The thing that weighed the least but mattered the most could never be used again.

Goddie cried as she walked up the gangplank to the open mouth in the side of the ship. Goddie Ormsby would walk onto the ship, but Veta Ormsby would have to walk off. The death of her name was the final reminder. Starting over meant even relearning how to use her own name. Everything she ever cared about now resided in her heart. Her name would take its place right beside her parents and her home in Spring Hill, Jamaica.

It would take another two hours to completely load the ship. Goddie watched from the observation deck as families were separated at one end and provisions were loaded at another. The Irpinia consumed its cargo hour by hour, bearing the burdens of strangers and the hopes of loved ones all in one sitting.

The view from the deck gave her a lasting look at Kingston. Her eyes scanned the horizon as the morning bell from the Half Way Tree clock rang out. Despite its treachery, Kingston was still a glorious city—a place of commodity sold by people who were commodities. It was the heartbeat of a land loved by its captives and exploited by its captors.

Goddie watched as the longshoreman sealed the mouth of the ship. She jumped when the Irpinia sounded three long horn blasts. It was time to be towed out of port. The moment was here. Still a little drenched, she reached into the sack to touch her documents and her Daadie's Bible. The Bible stayed dry. Over an hour of walking in the rain and the Bible didn't have a moist leaf.

*Thank you, Daadie. It's time for us to go now.*

Movement was happening. Goddie felt the ship labor forward as she watched the port move away from her. Loved ones onshore waved handkerchiefs and scarfs as a final goodbye. The smart ones waved bright colors so they could be seen easily. Goddie used her red headscarf to wipe her tears. There was no one to say goodbye to. No siblings to wave and no parents to console. She put her head down on the deck rail.

A clanging bell broke through the rush of waves and noise. Goddie lifted her head to see where it was coming from. Her ears scoured the air, and her eyes did the same, trying to find its owner. As the boat picked up speed, so did the search. She only had moments left before the boat cleared the port. She searched and searched, and finally, there he was. A lean man on a bicycle clanging a bell at the end of the port.

Mr. Hammil waved frantically, clanging his bell and waving a red scarf. Goddie locked eyes with her second father and pulled out her headscarf too. The pair waved and blew kisses with earnest. She couldn't see his eyes, but she saw him wipe his face with the scarf.

"Thank you. Thank you. Love yuh. Thank you, Mr. Hammil. Sorry," Goddie shouted with a desperate voice.

She threw both arms in the air and waved as the final curtain call on Jamaica closed. The port disappeared and, with it, so did Mr. Hammil—so did Lauretta, Lambert, Vurley, Lincoln, Dearis, Reynold, Minnette, and Lassie. They all disappeared on the horizon.

Just then, a strong breeze picked up on the observation deck. The deck cleared, and siddity maidens clutched their pearls, grabbed their headdress, and scurried inside. Not Goddie, she knew that breeze. She pressed off the railing and faced the bow as the morning breeze wrapped itself around its daughter one last time. Goddie closed her eyes and stretched out her arms. Her head tilted up as Jamaican glory bathed her one last time.

Goodbye, Jamaica.

## CHAPTER 26

# WINDRUSH BABY

---

The welcoming breeze Goddie was used to was now replaced with the stench of a thousand asses. The Caribbean air that wrapped her tight in Jamaica gave way to an itchy blanket in a cabin with no windows.

The compaction of West Indians within the berthing compartments of the ship bordered on criminal. The well-dressed Jamaicans boarding in Kingston would soon be joined by well-dressed Spaniards, Portuguese, and French.

"Southampton United Kingdom. All to disembark!" shouted the deck captain as he walked the cabin hall ringing a bell. One short horn blast confirmed it all.

After twenty-one days at sea, Goddie finally arrived in England. She rose from her bunk, brushed off the front of her dress, and quickly put her things together.

Working at Mr. Hammil's store for many years ingrained in her the importance of having her things organized and neat. It paid off as she quickly assessed her belongings and double-checked her travel instructions.

"Birth certificate, travel letter, and money," she whispered as she audited her papers. She couldn't afford to make a mistake. There would be no one to rescue her. Double-checking would prove lifesaving. She packed her belongings back into the small suitcase and arranged Daadie's Bible in her sack.

*We're here, Daadie. We're here.*

Her thoughts were broken as the sounds of excitement filled the air. She listened as grown men talked of promises of employment and better lives than the ones they left. For these men, this trip was the response to the request for more labor in the United Kingdom's transportation section. The government had opened up avenues for employment in public transportation and interregional transport.

Three things mattered to Goddie: catching the train to London, getting some food, and getting a coat. The weather in London was an unpleasant welcoming committee. She stared at the overcast skies from the hull opening. The howling winds coming off the English Channel were bone-crushing. The winds cut left to right. Goddie wrapped every piece of material she had around her body as she walked the gang-plank off the ship. The frigid waters mocked her as she tightened her fists and shivered her way to a new start. Grown men huddled around cans of fire as they figured out their next move.

"Papers, please." A small wisp of man looked through his horn-rimmed glasses at Goddie shivering.

She ran her hand across Daadie's Bible as she reached for her documents.

"V-E-T-A. How do you pronounce that, ma'am?" asked the officer.

Goddie responded through chattering teeth. "VEE-Tah." She was growing more comfortable saying her legal name out loud. It was a secret code—a name that could gain access to places Goddie couldn't go.

"Final destination?"

"Sir, the address is on the sponsor letter in front of you," replied Goddie.

"70 Maryland Road in London? That's over three hours from here. You had best get a coat if you want to survive in the United Kingdom, ma'am. Welcome to England."

The sound of the stamp hitting that letter was the best thing Goddie ever heard. It was the sound of new beginnings. The sound of the stamp was a starting pistol to the rest of her life. It was the sound of starting over. Through chattering teeth, she pressed a smile across her cold face and tucked her letter back beside Daadie's Bible.

The officer lifted his head and pointed with a pen. "There's a thrift shop on your way to the South Western Railway. It's a mile down the road. Get a coat before you get sick."

"Yes, sir," Goddie replied as she began walking in the direction of the train station.

Before long, Goddie had a new coat and had boarded the train to London. She was wrapped up tight as she settled in to watch the countryside pass by. Her eyes recorded the mundane as the train whisked across southern England. She recognized fellow travelers from the boat, and they were quick to smile and tip their hats.

With each greeting and with each smile, the understanding was made clear. All of them were there to make the most of the lightning they had caught in a bottle. They owed all those who suffered before them to make the most of this opportunity. They all began on their own starting line, and their future was highly dependent on the work they put in, the dedication they put forth, and the faith they exercised.

Everything was a new education. The South Western Railway, the tube station, and even walking down Warwick Avenue were all counted as an adventure. Her eyes lit up as she exited the Bakerloo Station and walked north. She stopped to admire the black nurses reporting for duty at St. Mary's Hospital. She stared at the black porters reporting for work at Paddington Station.

"Is this the way to Marylands Road?" she asked the local newsboy on the corner.

"I think it's farther up the road, ma'am."

"I'll show you. I'm headed that way," said a strange but familiar voice.

Goddie turned around to see a bundled-up Jamaican woman a little younger than her. Her nurse uniform peeked out from under her coat, and her shoes could belong to no other profession.

"You look like you just arrived. I'm Olive Williams."

"I'm Godd......I mean, I'm Veta." The women shook hands and walked north on Warwick Avenue.

"You're going to need a thicker coat if you're going to survive English winter, my dear," Olive suggested. She took off her wool scarf and wrapped it around Goddie's neck. She tucked the ends in Goddie's coat and grabbed her arm as the wind picked up. Olive knew what it was like to be new.

"Alright, Miss Veta. Tell me all about your boat ride. Was it as miserable as mine?" Olive burst out in the best belly laugh Goddie had ever heard. Olive's shoulders jumped up and down as she amused herself and her new friend. She threw her arm inside Goddie's, and the two proceeded up the street like old pals.

Goddie found Olive to be joy personified. What she lacked in height, she made up in friendliness and good nature. She was a psychiatric nurse at the local hospital and had already been in England for a few years. As they walked, Olive explained to Goddie how best to navigate the new world.

She discussed where to go, where not to go, and how to get into the nursing program.

Goddie soaked up each word like food itself. It felt good to have a friend.

After a short walk, Olive pointed down a street.

"Well, Veta, this is Marylands Road. A lot of us live on this road. It's much much better than the Notting Hill slums they put some of us in. I live up the road with my other nurse girl-friends. My boyfriend, Noel, comes by when he's not studying, so maybe we can all go out sometime," suggested Olive.

"I would love that. Oh, here's your scarf back."

Olive smiled. "You keep it, Veta. Consider it a welcome gift. Here's the phone number of the house where we stay. Welcome to England. Let me know if you need any help with school."

Goddie watched as her new friend walked up the street and around the corner. She reached down and patted the side of her sack with her father's Bible.

*She has the same laugh as you, Daadie.*

Goddie pulled out the letter with the address. She double-checked the street and walked down to the end. Before long, she was standing in front of the house. It was a brick building at the end of some row houses. A small white wall surrounded most of the property, and the front stairs led to a beautiful wood door with windows. The number seventy was prominent in brass.

As she stared at the house, Goddie became overwhelmed. She had come a long way. She had faced the worst of life's offerings. She accepted the moment. With her first step to the front door, she began her life over from the middle. She took her frozen hand out of her jacket and banged the knocker. A familiar shape appeared on the other side of the glass.

"Goddie?"

Goddie dropped her belongings as her friend grabbed her. Ann kissed both cheeks and wiped her friend's tears as Goddie fell into her arms. She had been carrying so much for so long. The two young women stood on the steps and wept at the idea of victory.

"I'm sorry…"

"No, Goddie. No more apologies. We are here now. We are together now. I made some soup. Welcome to England."

Ann grabbed her friend's bags, she grabbed her friend's hand, and the two entered the warmth of a house that had been awaiting this guest for too long.

# PART VI

# THE ARSONIST

## CHAPTER 27

# THE NURSE AND THE STRANGE FELLOW

———

The years after that first winter went quickly. The collage of classes and grades flowed down the stream of life as promised. Fetching water and tending to chickens gave way to physiology, biology, and psychology lectures. The assurance of hard work and sacrifice made good on its covenant with Goddie.

For the first half of her life, she had sowed in tears; now she was reaping in joy. England reshaped her and London thickened her blood. Knowledge sharpened her perception. She had learned more in twelve English winters than a lifetime in Spring Hill, Jamaica.

She felt like a woman now. A professional woman. An educated woman. A self-made woman. If trauma was the lesion, then progress was indeed the balm. The fragments of her pieces swept together to pave the most glorious path forward.

She had finally traded that green dress from Lauretta for a white one. The badge she wore no longer said *alone*. It read *nurse*.

After taking twelve years to perfect her skills in psychiatry and midwifery, she answered the call to go to Canada. The late sixties saw a significant need for health care workers, and she answered.

English nurses scattered themselves around the world to bring their skills to bear and venture into new horizons. Goddie was no different. If she was good at anything, she was good at starting over. Even in her mid-thirties, she still wanted more.

*Dear Veta,*

*I received your letter from Canada this week. I was so very glad to hear from you, and I am happy to know you are doing well. Life in London is going well, but I'm looking forward to seeing you in a few weeks. It's nice we are starting to get to know each other, and hopefully, we can get together when I move to Toronto in December. Ever since I saw your picture, I can't get you out of my mind. I am so looking forward to seeing you in person and getting to know you. I would like to stay with you when I come.*

*Christmas is coming. Can I bring you anything from London? Stay nice. Write soon.*

*Clinton*

Goddie held the letter with one hand and fried plantain with the other. A grease spot stained the corner of the letter, so she held it up to the light.

"November 11, Remembrance Day," she whispered. She tossed the letter to the side and continued her frying. "This guy is ridiculous. Something tells me I'm not going to want to remember him when this is over."

Apparently, Clinton saw Goddie's picture when he visited her friend Mona. Mona and her husband, Stennett, sold Clinton on Goddie.

Week after week, red-and-blue-striped letters arrived from Clinton wanting to talk. During nursing school, Goddie declined most offers to go out, preferring to stay in and focus on school. She had seen time and time again young nurses quit school because of some boy, and she vowed it wouldn't be her.

Clinton was persistent. His words coated her heart like toffee on a hot sidewalk. He was surgical in his courtship. Whatever he represented, it was nice to have a little attention.

After four more persistent weeks, Goddie agreed to see him. He arrived on her doorstep in early January 1970, and the relationship began. For her, it was nice to lean on a shoulder that wasn't her own. It was nice to talk about Jamaican life and feel a kinship with a man after her father.

When he smiled, his cheek bones became finite as his mustache and smile took center stage. His caramel skin gleamed when he talked. He was well-refined and completely put together. There was no doubt he was a gorgeous man. His light-brown eyes promised long life. He was libertine with his swagger.

Goddie fell for him. Eventually, she fell hard enough to marry him in the spring of 1970.

***

"Ring, Ring"

"Ring, Ring, Ring."

"I'll get it," Goddie yelled. She put down the knife and walked into the living room. She walked around the table and began to sit down next to the screaming telephone.

"No, no, no. I got it," Clinton said as he bounded out the bedroom, glided past the armchair, and sat at the end of the chesterfield. He did all that and picked up the receiver like it was a dismount from a balance beam.

"Hello?" Clinton crooned as Goddie sat at the other end of the chesterfield, looking right at him. His whole disposition changed. The hard lines in his face disappeared and whoever was on the line made his forehead glisten.

Seeking privacy from his wife, he picked up the receiver and base and dragged the telephone wire around the corner. The whistling kettle broke the shame as Goddie returned to the kitchen to finish dinner. As she served out the dinner, she heard keys jangling from hands getting ready to leave.

"I'll be back," he said as he walked past the kitchen without stopping.

That was the second night that week. They had only been married a few months, and he was acting like he wasn't married to anyone. Goddie knew she had made a mistake.

*Daadie, yuh see this lying, lecherous person? He charmed me from another country, married me, and now has dishonored me all in less than a year.*

Night after night, Goddie sat in the living room of the two-bedroom apartment, waiting for this coward to bring his defiled self home. Every night, he came home either chalked up with Appleton's finest rum or the perfume of some skettel woman. This evening would prove to be no different. Goddie sat on the chesterfield alone as her husband came in from his date.

"Why did you marry me?" she asked as she sat in the dark alone.

Clinton threw his keys on the living room table and trounced into the kitchen. His very presence was saturated with insufferable contempt. He fixed himself another drink, and the squeak of the ice in the glass announced his presence back to the living room.

"Whuh yuh want? Listen to me. Nuh baddah cross-question me. I'll answer to you when I want to and not before. I don't see any dinner. Yuh lucky I don't deal wid yuh fuh dat." Clinton jingled his glass and turned toward the bedroom.

Goddie bounced up and swung her monster around. "Just remember. As God knows, mark this day. I will nevah forgive yuh for dragging me into this gutter with yuh. Yuh is a wotless man. Yuh dug my ditch, but yuh just dug two fuh you." She shoved his drunk ass to the side and went into the bedroom. She locked the door behind her and slumped down on the floor with Daadie's Bible.

*Daadie, you see this wotless man! I've come this far, and I'm still carrying crosses. How can this be? This man is a curse upon the cursed. Wretched is the name of the one who loved under a lie and deceived under the guise of honor. This long life wore down all my instincts. I should have known better. I should have left his flowery words on the branch. Now, like the flower, I'm dying inside. Like a serpent, this man is squeezing me. He's squeezing me, Daadie.*

She removed her glasses and wiped her tears as she took stock of what she had allowed to enter her life.

Mumma's voice came clear to her as she sat in the corner. She recounted her advice about men and how "we should never mek dem turn us fool." Clinton was the antithesis of a man. He was mean for mean's sake—in all ways pathetic, in all ways a false friend, in all ways an adulterous husband. Months felt like years as this strange fellow with no compass led hearts to the hammer's block.

He was no Daadie. He was no Lambert. He was certainly no James.

He was an albatross. An unemployed, no skills, no respect, godless albatross.

Goddie pressed against the wall as she tried to get up. She could hear his drunken snoring in the next room. Infidelity can certainly wear a man out.

She exhaled hard as she held her back with one hand and her belly with the other.

The twins were kicking.

## CHAPTER 28

# IT ALL GETS REVEALED

---

The constant beeping was insufferable. "Is there any way to turn this down?" Goddie pleaded.

The only thing worse than the vital sound monitors was the parade of nurses and doctors. They were forever poking, prodding, and talking about what they needed to do to ensure the twins' safe delivery.

"I'll turn it down for you, Veta," replied Almeta.

Goddie had found a close friend in Nurse Almeta Rowe since they both migrated to Canada together. Almeta was now the charge nurse at Mt. Sinai hospital and was concerned about Goddie's progress. She flipped through her chart and examined Goddie's belly.

Like her marriage, attempting to carry twins in her early forties was a difficult experience. Goddie was on her second month of hospital bedrest. It wasn't clear what was worse— preeclampsia or death from boredom. Boredom was winning.

She had never been so still in her life. After years of farming, running, and migrating, she didn't know how to be still. Mt. Sinai Hospital was a great place to work but staring out the window watching the hours exhausted her soul. Her days of checking on patients and writing reports were replaced with counting dots on ceiling tiles and waiting for Clinton to show up.

"Is your husband coming to see you, Veta?" asked Almeta.

"What time is it?" Goddie inquired.

"It's six-thirty."

Goddie returned her stare out the window. Depending on Clinton was a fool's errand. She knew he had plenty of time to leave work and make his way to the hospital since Turnbull Elevator Factory, was only a few miles from the hospital.

A few months earlier, tired of his drunken state, she tried to get him a job at the factory. She asked her friend Alvin to try to get him on. Clinton had only been working there a few months when her bedrest was mandated.

Almeta left the room as the beeping started back up again. Goddie needed Clinton's support, and he was supposed to bring her another blanket and some dinner so she could take her medication.

Almeta rushed back in and went straight over to the window. The room was on the second floor, so she leaned on the windowsill and fixed her attention on the lower ground level. She stood there for a moment and then turned her eyes to Goddie.

"Veta, does your husband drive a brown Chevy with a blanket in the backseat?"

"Yes," Goddie replied. "That's the car he takes to work. He would be taking the bus if it wasn't for me. I took the loan on that car."

Almeta's jaw tightened as she fixed her stare and tapped her pen. She returned to Goddie's chart and finished documenting her medication changes. Silence swept the room. Goddie watched her nurse friend fluster through the chart and sensed the disturbance.

"What is it, Almeta?"

Nurse Rowe opened her mouth to speak but closed it and said, "Nothing."

"Almeta, I asked you a question. Answer me, please."

"Nurse Candace from trauma unit had been working downstairs all afternoon. She told me she finished her shift and just spent the last hour talking to this strange fellow in a brown chevy. He said he wasn't married and was here visiting his mother. He was asking all kinds of strange questions and wanted to…"

"Hi, Veta," greeted the strange fellow.

In came Clinton with his empty hands bounding over to place his Judas kiss on Goddie's cheek. Her eyelids crawled open slowly as she steadied herself for the performance.

"How was work? Looks like you worked late," Goddie said.

"Yeah, they have me working overtime. They like to work the new guy rough, so I had to put my time in. I'm just getting off now. I rushed right over."

Filled with indignation, Nurse Rowe looked over her glasses. He didn't have his wedding ring on, and Goddie knew in that moment a child could have made up a better lie.

"You said you just got off and came straight here?" Goddie questioned.

Nurse Rowe stopped writing just to hear the answer.

"Yeah. What happened?"

The lie filled the air as the two nurses watched the breakdown of the strange fellow.

"Nothing. Suh where's the food? Where's the blanket?" asked Goddie.

"I didn't have time. I came straight here. I could go for it now," Clinton replied.

Goddie scanned this wretched man and cussed herself. She scrolled her eyes down, looking for a wedding band. She knew the factory had rules about jewelry, which Clinton didn't seem too upset about.

She adjusted her position in the bed and stared out the window. The spring clouds of March released their cargo on a busy Toronto evening. Lightning flashed in the distance as the rain hit the hospital window. Clinton collected his things and stood up to leave.

"Soon come back," he decreed and went out into the hall and around the corner.

Almeta leaned in close to Goddie's ear. "Veta, I'm going to run down to the market and get you some dinner. Those twins need a meal." She squeezed her girlfriend's hand as Goddie hid her face in shame.

Within the hour, Almeta was back with some of Toronto's finest Jamaican food and a blanket. Goddie ate slowly as she watched the drizzle fall outside.

She knew what the rain meant.

# CHAPTER 29

# ARSONIST

———

"How do you feel, Veta?" asked Almeta.

Goddie couldn't answer. Her uterus was doing all the talking. She winced in pain as her uterus and cervix dictated terms. The pain shot through her like a cannon. The twins decided today was the day. Their premature status created a precarious situation, and everyone was waiting on Dr. Geddes for the word.

*What's going on?* she wondered. Moments of reprieve were broken by the piercing sound of the hall alarm.

The fire alarm screamed up and down the hallways of Mt. Sinai Hospital. A small fire on another floor sent patients out to University Avenue and the rest into the hallway. The stress of the alarm aggravated her labor.

She gripped the rails as they repositioned her body on the bed. It was suspected that one of the twins was experiencing an inguinal hernia, creating a stranglehold on his intestine. Prolonging the delivery due to the fire alarm would risk the viability of the babies.

A constriction of blood throughout the intestine needed attention. They had to be delivered and delivered quickly.

Dr. Geddes leaned over to Goddie and looked her straight in the eye. "Ok, Veta, we're going to have to go in and get these boys. We can't wait any longer."

Goddie nodded and looked around the room. Her eyes weaved in between the nurses trying to find Clinton, but he wasn't there. She knew deep down he was never planning on being there.

The beeping stopped as the nurses disconnected everything and threw another blanket on top of her. She reached over in the frenzy and rubbed Daadie's Bible on the stand just before she was pulled away. The fire alarm finally quieted as the nurses wheeled her down the hall.

Within a few hours, Goddie became a mother of two four-pound, premature twin boys.

The moment was lost on her as she struggled to sit up in bed. She swung her feet over the side of the bed and pressed to stand up. Her abdomen seized in pain as she willed herself down the hall to check on her boys.

"Hi, Veta. Congratulations," Almeta said as she ran with a wheelchair. "You should be resting. You had a big procedure."

"I'll rest when I see them," replied Goddie as she took a seat. Her friend wheeled her to the edge of the observation window, and Goddie quickly saw the first one.

He was wrapped up tight in the hospital's finest with a small beanie on his head. His chest moved up and down rapidly in the incubator as attendees took notes and checked monitors.

"Where's the other one?" she asked.

"They had to take him to the Sick Children's Hospital. He was having some difficulty with his bowels, and we needed to clear the obstruction and repair the hernia."

Goddie stared through Almeta. She looked back through the observation glass and gripped the wall. She was too weak to go anywhere.

"Who is with him?"

Almeta rubbed her back. "Oh, don't worry, Veta. Dr. Geddes went over with him. They'll do the hernia procedure over there and bring him back in few days. When is your husband coming?"

Goddie's face was resigned as the nurse's words bounced off the looking glass. She removed her horn-rimmed glasses and wiped the mucus from her nose. Her eyes glazed over as she shifted her weight and turned toward her friend.

"I don't think I have a husband anymore. A husband would have been here," Goddie whispered.

Almeta remained silent. Her eyes welled with tears for her friend. Goddie's heartbreak laid bare for all to see. After all, her body was too tired to mask anything. The two nurses stared through the observation glass.

"Take me back to my room, please," Goddie requested.

"Sure. Let's go, Veta," replied Almeta.

Goddie's friend pushed her down the hall back to her room. In a few days, she was released from the hospital with her sons.

\*\*\*

After a long six weeks, with the twins finally home, Goddie went back on nursing duty. The August summer breeze flowed differently outside East General Hospital. It flowed down Mortimer Avenue, through the parking lot, and across Goddie's lap like an aberrant brew.

She had been on her feet for nine hours. It had already been thirty minutes past the time Clinton promised he would pick her up at the hospital. Her jaw tightened as she read five-thirty on her small Quartz watch. She watched as the last rush-hour bus stopped to pick up passengers. Goddie looked down the road one last time and got on the bus.

The bus was packed like a tin of mackerel, and it smelled just the same. Goddie seethed at the idea that she was paying the loan on a vehicle she couldn't even ride in. Her enmity grew with each annoying stop. With mercy, the bus stopped a block short of Gamble Avenue. She pressed through the sea of stench and stepped out the rear of the bus. She turned toward her street and picked up the pace.

Goddie turned her head as a fire truck screamed up Pape Avenue. She walked farther down and turned on Gamble Avenue toward the apartment. Finally, the back tail lights of the brown Chevy came into view. She was confused. The license plate was hers, but it didn't make sense.

The closer she got, the clearer the silhouette of the woman became. She had a jet-black upsweep hairdo rolled to the side. Her high cheekbones poked out from the side and her right arm glistened as it rested on the open door window.

"What in wor...," Goddie whispered. She walked alongside the car. The stranger looked comfortable, like she was used to riding in that seat.

Goddie thought better of it and left her alone. She turned, brushed off the front of her uniform, and pulled her key for the lobby door.

The elevator opened quickly, and she took the ride to the ninth floor alone. Goddie swallowed with each passing floor number. She stepped out and proceeded down the hall. The sound of rubbing polyester filled the hall as her bag rubbed her uniform.

Within steps, she was at her front door. Goddie fumbled with the key as she negotiated with the lock. The latch turned, and she pressed the door open. Clothes and personal items were strewn everywhere. A bathroom bag sat on the edge of the coffee table. Goddie swallowed hard and exhaled.

"Did we have pest control spray the apartment today?"

"No," Clinton responded as he rounded the corner with two suitcases. One of them was Goddie's. He walked past her and opened one of the cases on the coffee table.

"Where are you going, Clinton?"

"I'm leaving," he replied.

"Leaving? Leaving to go where?" Goddie stepped in between his packing.

His eyes were clear and lucid. His facial expression hinted at how long he had been planning to light this fire. His lips and jawline kept their discipline. They gave away no secrets.

"These babies of yours are keeping me awake. I can't sleep. I need to go where I can get some sleep," Clinton whined.

"Are these not your babies as well? You didn't create them?" Goddie questioned.

Clinton continued to load his suitcases.

"You can't sleep? So can't the millions of fathers who have new babies at home. What makes you so different? It's called life. It's called being a man," shouted Goddie.

The more she talked, the faster he packed.

"You were just going to leave? Leave me at the hospital and leave the boys in their crib?"

He threw the last few pieces in the suitcase. The snap of clicking latches was the match. Clinton slung a bag across his body and grabbed each suitcase. Like an arsonist, he swung the apartment door open and looked back at what he had just set on fire. Arsonists like that part. They like to watch it all burn.

Goddie's eyelids crawled open to address him again. She decided not to.

"You'll be ok. Canada is good to women." With that, he turned and walked out of the apartment and down the hall.

Her husband of seventeen months left his black twin boys for a black upsweep and glistening arms.

Goddie stared into thin air as the sound of the elevator doors echoed in the hallway. She walked over to the balcony, opened the screen door, and gripped the railing tight while inching herself into view of where the Chevy was parked.

Clinton loaded Goddie's bags into Goddie's car and pulled off into the summer night.

She watched as the arsonist left her in the fire.

Goddie stepped back into the apartment. With the boys screaming, she collapsed on the floor.

## CHAPTER 30

# DAADIE'S SMILE

---

The weeks between Clinton leaving and Goddie healing were difficult. The August heat smothered the Gamble Avenue apartment. Humidity thickened the air, sucking the energy of even the well-intended. The oscillating fan on the coffee table worked triple overtime, sharing relief between Goddie and the boys in the crib.

The stress of a broken marriage was minuscule to the reality of having to raise two babies by herself. She was in a new country with no husband, no car, and no family—all while watching half the household income disappear.

"Come on, Veta. Try this tea," begged Donna.

Donna had come straight over to the apartment after her shift at the hospital. She and Goddie worked in the ninth-floor post-surgery department. Donna and the rest of Goddie's nursing friends were fighting to get her well.

Goddie stared blankly at the swirling liquid in the cup. She had spent the last several days in bed recovering from exhaustion.

Her girlfriends and colleagues came to the apartment in shifts to take care of her and keep an eye on the twins. She spent her days staring out the window, swatting flies, and debating whether today was the day she would bathe. Nevertheless, life was carrying on around her.

The mail piled high and unopened. All the envelopes with her name on them were marked PAST DUE. Embarrassment colored every action she took. Shame was too easy a description. She allowed this arsonist of a man into her life and watched as he burned what she had built to the ground.

"Donna, I'm not really hungry," Goddie whispered as she let the cup slide off the saucer.

Donna reached down to catch the falling teacup. Her heart confirmed what her mind already knew. Goddie was depressed. Goddie was traumatized. The sound of bottles boiling on the stove broke Donna's concentration.

"I think the bottles are sterilized now. I'll get them," said Donna.

Goddie's eyes crawled from the floor up to where Donna stood. She slowly nodded her approval and returned her gaze to the floor. Somehow counting the shag strands on the carpet took her mind off her realities.

Goddie didn't know a man could treat her that way. For her entire life, her heart was granted safe harbor when she dealt with men. Whether it was James, Lambert, or even Daadie, every one of them was a prince. The thought of them being hurtful or abusive didn't exist. All that changed with Clinton.

A knock on the apartment door broke Goddie's attention. She shifted her weight to get up just as Donna came out of the kitchen.

"Sit down, Veta. I got it," commanded Donna. She approached the door and looked through the peek hole.

"Who is it?" inquired Donna.

"This is Alvin. Just coming to check in on Veta," the voice replied.

Donna looked over at Goddie, who nodded her approval. The door was opened, and a tall, fair-skinned gentleman filled the doorway. His hands were filled with groceries as he stepped across the threshold into the apartment.

Goddie's face lit up when she saw her old friend.

"I'm going to put these bags in the kitchen for you, Veta," said Alvin.

He quickly placed the bags on the counter and made his way over to his friend. Donna proceeded to unpack the bags. As Alvin approached, the sound of babies interrupted his stride. He looked over to see four eyes looking back at him from the crib.

The twins were awake and looking for action. He stared down at the boys for a long time. He rested one hand on the crib and adjusted their blanket with the other.

"Veta, I'm so sorry this happened to you. I feel ashamed as a man. You didn't deserve this. When I think about how you fought for this...m...."

"Don't worry about it. Come and sit down," interrupted Goddie as she waved him over and moved the cushions off to the side.

Alvin sat beside his friend and gave her a hug. She closed her eyes and leaned on him for a few seconds. After a few rough weeks, it felt good to hear a friendly male voice. Another knock came on the door.

"Veta, this is beginning to feel like Union Station," quipped Donna. She looked through the peephole again.

"Who is it?" inquired Donna.

"This is Almeta Rowe. Just coming to check in on Veta," the voice replied.

Donna opened the door again. Almeta smiled at Goddie and headed directly over to the crib. Her prenatal nurse training kicked in as she picked up the smallest baby.

"Veta, Robert looks like he's gained weight," Almeta said.

"Yes, he's starting to fill out now," Goddie replied.

Robert was the youngest and the smallest of her boys. His hernia surgery was successful, but Almeta wanted to keep an eye on him.

She checked the scar on his abdomen and pinned his diaper before returning him to the crib. Almeta picked up Richard next. As she checked him over, he spat up all over her uniform.

"This one is going to be a rough one," Almeta said, laughing. "It's a good thing I was on my way home."

She returned Richard to his side of the crib, grabbed a wet rag, and took a seat across from Goddie. The mood of the apartment reverted to solemn as Goddie's marriage status suddenly held center court.

"Alvin, is he still showing up for work?" inquired Goddie.

"Yes, Veta. He hasn't missed a day."

Alvin looked down as he rubbed his feet together. Goddie watched as he became more and more uncomfortable.

"Something on your mind?" Goddie inquired.

Alvin looked down again. He sighed deeply as he rubbed his hands together and looked at the crib. All the stalling now had everyone's attention. Almeta, Donna, and the twins waited for Alvin to get it together.

"You are going to have some problems with him, Veta," Alvin stated.

"What do you mean?" Goddie replied.

"Clinton and I were drinking the other night. It took half a bottle of Wray and Nephew before he started blabbing his mouth off. When I asked him about you, he went on and on about having other babies with other women. He mentioned having twin girls in England, but I'm not sure if it was just the rum talking."

"Go on," requested Goddie.

She stared out the apartment window as the sky retired for the evening. None of this information was surprising to her. Arsonists and sociopaths like to destroy things and brag. Her psychiatry training helped her make sense of the past few weeks. It wouldn't feed the babies, but it would confirm that she wasn't the crazy one.

Alvin explained further. "He showed me pictures of some older kids. A boy and a girl. They looked about ten and twelve and fair-skinned just like him. When I asked him how he supports all these kids, he kissed his teeth and took another drink. The rum did the talking for the remainder of the night. I'm sorry, Veta. I just thought you deserved to know. It hurts me to even have to tell you," Alvin said, sighing.

"That's alright," Goddie replied, patting his leg. She rubbed her hands together and started to cry. She rotated the wedding band on her finger as she looked out the window.

The silence was deafening. She took a handkerchief from under her lap and wiped her nose. She was tired of crying and exhausted from grieving.

Almeta made some curry chicken, and Donna whipped up some oxtails to hold Goddie over. Alvin cleaned up the apartment, took out the trash, and wiped down the counters. Goddie finally got up from the chesterfield to say goodbye to her friends.

"Wow. If I knew I could get all this cooking and cleaning, I would have kicked Clinton out sooner," she said, laughing as she tried to lighten the mood.

"Thank you, everyone. We'll be ok. God is watching," she said as her friends made their way down the hall to the elevator.

Almeta turned back, pulling out a plastic shopping bag from her purse.

"I almost forgot to give you this mail I picked up on the way in. It looks like there are a few important envelopes, so be sure to open them," Almeta said. She kissed Goddie on the cheek, handed her the bundle, and scurried onto the waiting elevator.

Goddie closed the door and returned to the chesterfield. Sorting the envelopes was a welcomed distraction despite the pile being mostly past-due bills. Her face brightened as she got down to the last two envelopes.

The first letter was from the Immigration and Citizenship Canada office. The second letter was from Minnette.

She adjusted her glasses and read the first letter:

*In reference to your Canadian permanent residency application for Edith Ormsby...we are pleased to approve your application and request you proceed with...*

Goddie read the letter five more times. She had applied to sponsor her sister Lassie to come to Canada five years prior. For the last two years, she had received no communication from the government and had all but given up hope of reuniting with her sister. It hurt Goddie to leave her behind, but she never forgot her.

Goddie sat back as hope washed over her. She stared at the ceiling as seeds of restoration took root in her soul. She knew it would be a long road ahead, but Daadie was still watching.

The crack of the evening sky broke her gaze. She jumped up to close the balcony door as the heavens released their showers. She leaned against the glass door, smiling to herself. She knew what the rain meant. She brushed off the front of her housedress and placed her head on the glass door. Her thoughts began to take flight.

*Daadie, it's been a long journey. Many hurts along the way. But we are still here. You're still watching. You are sti...*

The rustling in the crib broke her moment. Robert tossed around as he cried for his mother. Richard stayed asleep in the commotion. The sutures from Robert's surgery were still fresh, so she thought they might need attention. His eyes locked on her as she reached in to pick him up. All the fussing and crying stopped.

"There's nothing wrong with you, Robert. I was talking to your grandfather, and you interrupted me," Goddie teased. She poked his belly, trying to get him to smile. She poked and poked. Nothing.

*He's stubborn just like you, Daadie.*

Robert suddenly turned his head and spread the biggest smile across his face. The last time she saw that smile, Goddie was with Daadie.

In her heart, she still is.

# ORMSBY FAMILY PHOTOS

**Missing Photos**
**Parents:** Christopher Ormsby, Caroline Ormsby
**Siblings:** Lambert Ormsby, Lauretta Ormsby

# ORMSBY FAMILY TREE

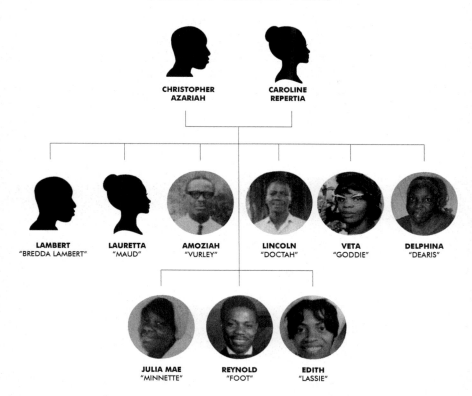

CHRISTOPHER AZARIAH

CAROLINE REPERTIA

LAMBERT
"BREDDA LAMBERT"

LAURETTA
"MAUD"

AMOZIAH
"VURLEY"

LINCOLN
"DOCTAH"

VETA
"GODDIE"

DELPHINA
"DEARIS"

JULIA MAE
"MINNETTE"

REYNOLD
"FOOT"

EDITH
"LASSIE"

# A TWIN'S EPILOGUE

---

Our story began at Mount Sinai Hospital. As premature babies, the doctors saved our lives, and Veta "Goddie" Picart taught us how to live them. What she sowed into us was special—a unique version of pride, the chin up, shoulders back, shoes clean kind of pride.

The early days for Robert and I were difficult. It was just the three of us, so we learned pretty early to bind together. Laughter was the fragrance in our home. That's pretty much all we had. It was enough though. Together, we believed nothing couldn't be overcome with a little humor and some faith.

Nevertheless, Goddie gave us what was given to her—a relationship with God. Robert and I gathered around the foot of her bed every Friday evening to usher in the Sabbath. We would nod off as her crackling voice exalted one Bible principle over another. We sometimes fell asleep during her long prayers, but we were always on time for the "Amen" at the end.

She gave us Toronto. Kensington Market remains etched in my mind—a proper market with fish on ice, hanging meat, and fresh hard dough bread. It was all there. We knew when it was payday because she would stop to get some handmade

Jamaican beef patties and a chubby soft drink on the way home. That was life.

Goddie could give a master class on financial management. Live a little, save a lot. She had a late start, but she finished strong. A single parent owning her own home was a rare bird in those days. We weren't rich, but we never lacked. There was always rainy-day money.

If mom was a superhero, then education was her cape. She didn't play around with school grades. She showed us that learning and education were not the same things. Whether it was getting her driver's license in her fifties or unwrapping her second iPad in her nineties, she didn't have a problem learning new things.

Goddie never forgot her family. For years, we watched mum pack barrels of packaged goods for Jamaica. Robert and I would take turns sitting on the lids of the shipping barrels just so she could stuff in that last bar of soap. Even today, when I visit her, as I put my hand on the door handle to leave, she's still asking, "Rich, you want an orange?"

They called her "Sister P" at church because when she wasn't working, cooking, gardening, or nursing, she was worshipping. That meant we were worshipping too. We took that Mortimer 62 bus to the Toronto East SDA church for years. Church attendance was like the postal service. It didn't matter the conditions. Rain, sleet, wind, or hail, our behinds were always in church.

She wrapped us with a church family that could stand in the gap when she couldn't. Mom taught us that we are all part of the family of God, no matter our religion. She taught us how to forgive, how to be honest, and how to be kind.

The definition of family extended to our friends. They say blood is thicker than water, but it's still 90 percent water.

Robert and I still treasure the influences of the men who gave us the guard rails of love, faith, and respect. Shout out to Uncle George McIntosh, Moses St. Juste, Uncle Enos Stewart, and a whole host of others who stood in the gap. We became what we saw. Thank you.

Mom is navigating the sunset of her life now. She's less guarded. She's spilling the beans now. I don't think Robert would ever have gotten the background for this book even just a few years ago.

It's funny how her memory is dull for recent events and razor sharp for things that happened seventy years ago. I have to speak louder when we talk. She refuses to wear a hearing aid, so I've traded in our banter for loud, short sentences. It's like talking to a Jamaican Alexa.

Goddie's legacy is secure. Her grandchildren Kehla, Kiara, Malachi, and Madison have replaced the flowers she used to grow in her front yard. She loved gardening. Watching things she loved fade out of her life was a familiar thing, except the flowers. They always came back.

Thank you, mom, for giving us the best of Veta and Goddie. Well done.

Gwaan, Goddie, big up yuh self.

Richard Picart

# ACKNOWLEDGMENTS

———

Writing a book sounds like a romantic idea until you get knee-deep and realize you can't do it alone. My gratitude extends far beyond the constraints of this page.

To my mom, Veta "Goddie" Picart, thank you. I know it was painful to relive some of the stories. Thank you for trusting me.

Special thanks to my wife Susan and my children, Malachi and Madison. I wrote this for you. It's hard to know where you are going if you don't know where you came from.

To my twin brother Richard, thank you. We finally got mom's story down on paper. Special thanks to Heather, Kehla, and Kiara for the ongoing support. To my siblings, Angela and Jimmy, thank you for the support.

I would like to acknowledge The Picart Family, The Ormsby Family, The Taylor Family, The Samuels Family, and The Rowe Family.

To Keisha-Marie Clarke, thank you for the support. You came through big time! I'll meet you at the Summer Suede Lounge!

To my cousin Bridgette Allen, you were pivotal to the very existence of this book. I'll see you soon.

To my friends and family in Toronto, Memphis, and Atlanta, thank you for the messages and words of encouragement.

Charisse Williams, I would not be typing these acknowledgments if it wasn't for you. Thank you.

A special thanks goes to Professor Eric Koester and the New Degree Press team. Special love goes to my editing team, Katie Sigler, Tasslyn Magnusson, and the wonderful Alayna Eberhart. Thank you for being patient with me.

What can I say about my beta readers? These wonderful people took the time to read chapter after chapter. Thank you for giving me honest feedback:

Andaleeb Syed, Andrea Ingleton-Smith, Ann Marie Donaldson, Ashante Infantry, Charisse Williams, Chloe Memoir, Emily Skaar, Grace Clarke, Heather Picart, Lisa Brown Alexander, Marla Hunter, Renee Rowe, Sharifa Walker, Stacey Campbell Marshall, and Susan Cameron.

Special thanks to Sandy Picart Thompson.

Last, but not least, I would like to thank the supporters who backed the book. After a two-minute video, you decided to join the journey. My thanks cannot be measured.

Aleece Germano
Amos Raymond
Andaleeb Dobson
Andrea Ingleton-Smith
Angela Samuels
Anthony Losurdo
Ashante Infantry
Bernadette Arthur
Candace Cabbil
Candace Doby
Carol Persaud
Carolee Miller
Caroline Bohm
Cathy Hulbert

Cawanea Young
Charisse Williams
Dana Baptist
Dani Leger
Darin Bohm
Deirdra Royston
Derrick Pratt
Derrick Pryce
Donald McLeod
Eiko Harris
Elianna Samuels
Elizabeth Wagner
Emily Skaar
Eric Koester

Eric Lange
Francis Sealy
Grace Clarke
Harold Flemming
Heather Picart
Honor Sylvester
Joanna Cole
Joelle Reuer
Josh Clegg
Joy Davis
Kathy Skoubouris
Keisha Smith
Keisha-Marie Clarke
Kevin Cameron
Keyeana Jones
Leena Sharma Seth
Len Carby
Lily Taylor
Lisa Brown Alexander
Lisa Rico
Madison Picart
Marcia Lake
Marcia Hunter
Mark Nelson
Matt Mashburn
Matthew West
Mellissa Davis
Mirthell Mitchell
Nathaniel Anderson
Nellene Jones
Newton Ormsby
Nifemi Aluko
Oretta Murray

Patricia Lewis
Patrick Caruso
Paul Samuels
Paul Starks
Philip Dugonjic
Peter Hunter
Rae-Vaughn Lucas
Ralph Johnson
Reginald Clark
Renee Rowe
Richard Hartman
Richard Picart
Robin Callender
Robin Houck
Rodger Muschett
Rosemarie Davis
Sandy Picart Thompson
Sharifa Walker
Shaundra Glass
Sheila Pryor
Stephan Boston
Stephanie Li
Susan Carlevaris
Susan Picart
Tamika Hunter
Tasha Holloway Gibbs
Tasslyn Magnusson
Temra Taylor
Tennille Thomas
Terry Emehel
Thomas Simmons
Tommy Laudig

# JAMAICAN GLOSSARY WORDS AND PHRASES

—

### WHAT IS PATOIS?

Patois is an English-based creole language spoken primarily in Jamaica. Its origins are traced back to West African influences. Below are a few common words and phrases used throughout the island, both in Goddie's era and continuing today.

| Jamaican Words | English Translation |
| --- | --- |
| Aks | Ask |
| Bless Up | Best wishes |
| Dash weh | To throw something away |
| Di | The |
| Dweet | Do it |
| Fiah | Fire |
| Galang | Leave me alone. |
| Gweh | Go away. |
| Irie | Everything is alright. |
| Mek | Make |

| | |
|---|---|
| Nuh | No, now, or know |
| Nyam (nee-ahm) | To eat. Mek wi nyam. (Let's eat.) |
| Rhaatid | Damn |
| Tallawah | To be strong |
| Weh yah guh | Where are you going? |
| Wutless | Worthless |

| Jamaica Expressions | English Translation |
|---|---|
| A wah duh dem, Goddie? | What's wrong with them, Goddie? |
| Ah suh di ting tan, Goddie. | That's the way it is, Goddie. |
| Big tings a gwaan, Goddie. | Great things are happening, Goddie. |
| Big up yuhself, Goddie. | Congratulate yourself, Goddie. |
| Bruck out | To misbehave |
| Deh suh it deh, Goddie. | That's where it's at, Goddie. |
| Easy nuh? | Chill out. |
| Everything is everything | All is well. |
| Goddie, dis ah big people ting. | Goddie, this is adult business. |
| Inna di morrows, Goddie | See you tomorrow, Goddie. |
| Kibba yuh mouth, Goddie. | Keep your mouth quiet, Goddie. |
| Likkle more, Goddie | See you later, Goddie. |
| Mi soon come. | I'll be right there. |
| Seet yah, Goddie. | Here it is, Goddie. |
| Stop rampin, Goddie | Stop playing, Goddie. |
| Try a ting | Try something. |
| U zeemi, Goddie? | Do you see what I'm saying, Goddie? |
| Wat a gwaan, Goddie? | What's going on, Goddie? |
| Weh yah guh, Goddie? | Where are you going, Goddie? |
| Weh yuh deh pon, Goddie? | What are you up to, Goddie? |
| Yah, mon. | Yeah, man. |